The Gospel of Jesus Christ:

The Truth, Teachings

and

Prophecy of the Messiah.

Contents

Dedication		3
Introduction		5
Chapter 1	The Gospel	8
Chapter 2	Social Issues	115
Chapter 3	False Teachings	164
Chapter 4	End Times Prophecy	199
Chapter 5	The Redemption of Man	285
Chapter 6	Accepting Jesus Christ	293
About the Author		295

Dedication

This book would never have been possible without the inspiration instilled in me by my Dad, Roosevelt Summerville, and Mom, Henredita Summerville. As a boy, my Father taught me a simple but powerful prayer, the Lord's Prayer referenced in Matthew 6:9-13 (NKJV). The scripture reads:

In this manner, therefore, pray: Our Father in heaven, Hallowed be thy name. Your kingdom come, your will be done, on Earth as it is in heaven. Give us this day our daily bread. And forgive us our debts, as we forgive our debtors. And do not lead us into temptation, but deliver us from evil. For thine is the kingdom, and the power, and the glory forever. Amen.

As a child, this had little meaning to me, but it meant the world to my Dad. As I grew and matured in the faith and into a man, this prayer sparked a flame within my Spirit that became a roaring blaze for Jesus Christ. In short, I can only thank the man who guided me to Christ by dedicating this book to Him. I Love You, Dad. Rest in Peace….

Introduction

The Christian faith is often plagued by a very simple question. Why do we as human beings need to accept Jesus Christ? The answer to this question revolves around the idea that "we are all sinners and are in need of a Savior." In many cases, this can cause non-believers to embrace repentance and acceptance of the Lord. It could also lead non-believers to reject His love and grace. Many times the question that is supplied is not sufficient to lead one to ask for Salvation. This book will help by providing Christians with fundamental answers pertaining to the Faith.

In this book, we will explore the reason for the gospel, and how man came to be in need of a perfect savior to free us from sin and please God the Father. The teachings of the cross of Christ are the single greatest body of knowledge any man or woman can speak to another person. The power and liberty possessed by those who have Faith is truly remarkable once they have received the word. This power will be examined and thoroughly explained throughout the reading this book. Romans 1:16 (NKJV) states: "For I am not ashamed of the gospel of Christ, for it is the power of God to salvation for everyone who believes, for the Jew first and also for the Greek." This scripture should rest on the hearts of all believers in the cross of Christ.

This writing will look at current social issues and how the Bible has predicted and supplied the answers to all mankind's questions. In retrospect, we will also examine many current false teachings in the Church today. This will provide the truth to what false doctrine means and what its intended purpose is to do in the Body of Christ. *The Gospel of Jesus Christ: The Truth, Teachings and Prophecy of the Messiah* will examine end times prophecy and many unfamiliar facts of the Holy Bible that are unknown to the majority of Christians.

We will also clarify the old question of why people should trust the Gospel. Many topics, such as the Gospel, Social Issues, False Teachings, End Times Prophecy and Little Known Facts about the scriptures, will be examined for their contributions to the need for the Gospel of Jesus Christ. I pray that each and everyone who has been purposed to read this book is truly blessed, and will share with others the knowledge of the Cross of Jesus Christ. Shalom…

Chapter 1

The Gospel

For I am not ashamed of the gospel, because it is the power of God that brings salvation to everyone who believes.

The gospel accounts recorded in the New Testament of the Holy Bible describe the life, times and events of Jesus Christ, the Son of God. The fulfillment of prophecy in the Old Testament documented a savior who would save those who believed in him from sin and death. The title of Messiah was given to Him for the position He would play as a Liberator for every man and woman to live a perfect life according to the will of God. Christ was sinless on Earth and upheld the perfect Law of Moses given from God. The Law of Moses required strict adherence. This included total submission to God's will such that no human being could keep without falling into some type of sin.

The law was necessary to reveal mankind's sin. Romans 7:7 (NKJV), reads: "What shall we say then? Is the law sin? Certainly not! On the contrary, I would not have known sin except through the law. For I would not have known covetousness unless the law had said, 'You shall not covet.'" The Law of Moses revealed that every man and woman is a sinner. No matter how upright a person walks, sinful nature exists within every creature on Earth. Due to the nature of sin, no one can keep the law that represents the original nature of man before the fall, as recorded in the book of Genesis. Often when we explain the Gospel and the need for repentance, we tend to overlook the original story of how exactly we, as Human Beings, were corrupted by Satan. Sin is an inherited trait from Adam and Eve, passed down through the bloodline of Humanity from one generation to the next. To better understand this point, it's helpful to examine the Katabole, which occurred in a distant past.

Lucifer's Flood (The Katabole)

For this they willfully forget: that by the word of God the heavens were of old, and the earth standing out of water and in the water, by which the world that then existed perished, being flooded with water. But the heavens and the earth which are now preserved by the same word, are reserved for fire until the day of judgment and perdition of ungodly men.— 2 Peter 3:5-7 (NJKV)

"Lucifer's flood" is another name for the fall of Satan, which took place in the Pre-Adamic Age. This is the Age that existed before God created Man. The Apostle Peter states that in the beginning, when the Earth was first formed, a cataclysmic event happened between Genesis 1:1 and 1:2. This caused the Earth to become void and formless while also causing the extinction of Life on this planet by having the sun blocked out by God. The record of the Earth is billions of years old and divided into three Earth Ages. The first was a time when Lucifer was in the Heaven and the second is the current reality we live in. The third Age will come with Christ's return. The Katabole represents a judgment of the social system at that time resulting in the Lord destroying all life. Whenever God blocks out the sun or causes darkness to fall on the land – as in Genesis 1:2 – this is always the result of judgment (see Gen 6-8, Ex 10:21, Jer 4:23, Joel 2:31, Rev 6:12, 8:12, 9:2, 16:10). This was the judgment of Satan when He rebelled against God. This is recorded in Ezekiel 28:13-17 (NKJV) and reads:

You were in Eden, the garden of God;
Every precious stone was your covering: The

sardius, topaz, and diamond, beryl, onyx, and jasper, Sapphire, turquoise, and emerald with gold. The workmanship of your timbrels and pipes was prepared for you on the day you were created. You were the anointed cherub who covers; I established you; You were on the holy mountain of God; You walked back and forth in the midst of fiery stones. You were perfect in your ways from the day you were created, Till iniquity was found in you. By the abundance of your trading You became filled with violence within, And you sinned; Therefore I cast you as a profane thing Out of the mountain of God; And I destroyed you, O covering cherub, From the midst of the fiery stones. "Your heart was lifted up because of your beauty; You corrupted your wisdom for the sake of your splendor; I cast you to the ground, I laid you before kings, That they might gaze at you.

This judgment caused the Earth to fall into chaos and destroyed utterly all life forms at that time. This was true until Man was created in Genesis 1:26 and empowered to replenish the Earth in Genesis 1:28. Many people overlook the fact that God said to *replenish* the Earth, meaning that something had to be here before Adam, which Satan's fall destroyed. The flood of 2 Peter 3:5-7 wiped all life from Earth, causing the need for the world to have to be remade by Adam some time later. This is where the Holy Bible picks up with starting in Genesis. The Earth that was created billions of years ago was in need of remodeling, which God ordained Man to do. God the Father once again made the Earth over, restoring life to the ravaged world impacted by the revolt of Satan in the Heavens. Every plant, animal, man and woman was perfect in God's image until corruption once again crept in.

The Serpent Seed

And I will put enmity between you and the woman, and between your seed and her Seed; He shall bruise your head, and you shall bruise His heel. – Genesis 3:15, (NKJV)

One of the most important but overlooked facts in the Holy Bible is that of the serpent seed. The original tale of Genesis symbolically alludes to separate bloodlines for Cain and Abel. As believers, it's important to be clear about exactly what happened in the Garden of Eden between Eve and the Serpent. We all know that "trees" represent people or kingdoms many times in the Bible which is prevalent throughout the New Testament. The two trees mentioned in the Garden – the "Tree of Life" and the "Tree of Knowledge of Good and Evil" – represent the Kingdom of God (Tree of Life) and one of Satan's (Good and Evil.) The Serpent in the Garden was used as a pawn in Satan's game to corrupt the bloodline of man, seeing as how God gave so much power unto man, who Satan saw as weaker than heavenly beings, used the serpent to seduce Eve. Genesis 3:13 (NKJV) says, "And the Lord God said to the woman, what is this that thou hast done? And the woman said, the serpent deceived (beguiled) me, and I did eat."

The word *beguiled* means to entrap or seduce, such as when Eve partook in the sinful nature of Satan and gained awareness of sexual knowledge. In return this same knowledge was made aware unto Adam shortly thereafter. The fruit of the tree of "Knowledge of Good and Evil" was not the literal fruit we eat today. Instead it represented all forms of sin, including sexual promiscuity. This sexual act between Eve and the Serpent angered God, who cursed Eve, such that in her infidelity she would now bring forth children. According to Genesis 3: 16 (NKJV), "To the woman he said, I will greatly multiply your sorrow and your conception; in pain you shall bring forth children;

your desire shall be for your husband, and he shall rule over you."

If Eve's only sin was eating a piece of fruit, why would God punish Eve with child-bearing? This is because Adam and Eve were given sexual knowledge before they were permitted to know. They brought forth sin and an ungodly bloodline through the Serpent. Satan was able to inject his nature into the human race by corrupting Adam and Eve, from whom we inherit our genetic traits. At the conception and birth of Cain, Eve knew immediately that Adam was not his Father. According to Genesis 4:1 (NKJV): "And Adam knew Eve his wife; and she conceived, and bore Cain, and said, I have acquired a man from the Lord." From the first look of Eve, Cain knew he was different. He wrongfully claimed he was from God, misinterpreting Genesis 3:15 (see above). Eve thought that this "special" child was a gift from God, but was the fraternal twin of Abel through the serpent. Cain took on all the murderous and deceitful attributes of His father Satan, murdering Abel and lying to God. Cain fled to the Land of Nod, where he married and produced other children, further spreading the serpent seed through the human gene pool.

The scriptures follow Cain's bloodline until Genesis 4:16-24 . The Bible begins from there, recording the new son Seth. The Bible story continues on from there. Why is this? Because Cain was not the son of Adam and not in the original creation which God began. More proof of this is offered in the genealogies of the origins of man in Genesis Chapter 5, Chronicles Chapter 1, and Luke Chapter 3:23-38. Cain is absent from these records because he was not from the offspring of Adam. So what became of Cain and his lineage? This bloodline continued in their wicked ways during the time of Christ and the Apostle Paul. Jesus stated in John 8:37-47 (NKJV), "I know that you are Abraham's descendants, but you seek to kill Me because My word has no place in you. I speak what I have seen with My Father, and you do what you have seen with your father. "They answered and said to Him, "Abraham is our father." Jesus said to them, "If you were Abraham's children, you would do the works of Abraham. But now you seek to kill Me, a Man who has told you the truth which I heard from God. Abraham did not do this. You do the deeds of your father. Then they said to Him, "We were not born of fornication; we have one Father – God." Jesus said to them:

> *If God were your Father, you would love Me, for I proceeded forth and came from God; nor have I come of Myself, but He sent Me. Why do you not understand My speech? Because you are not able to listen to My word. You are of your father the devil, and the desires of your father you want to do. He was a murderer from the beginning, and does not stand in the truth, because there is no truth in him. When he speaks a lie, he speaks from his*

own resources, for he is a liar and the father of it. But because I tell the truth, you do not believe Me. Which of you convicts Me of sin? And if I tell the truth, why do you not believe Me? He who is of God hears God's words; therefore you do not hear, because you are not of God.

John also stated this in 1 John 3:12 (NKJV),"Not as Cain, who was of that wicked one, and murdered his brother. And why did he murder him? Because his works were evil, and his brother's righteous."

This serpent seed continues today now in the realm of politics, religion and secret organizations that spread false doctrine and lies to the world. The sons of Cain are preparing the way for the world to accept the Anti-Christ. It is important to know why many human beings in their nature are so evil and deceitful at times. That is in the distant past, Deceit, murder and corruption entered in through Adam and Eve and the serpent seed.

The condition of mankind after this significant event was crippling to our Heavenly nature. In the fall of man, we lost everything God placed in us in order to have perfect Holy communion with Him. The Bible lists these shortcomings that altered Adam and Eve genetically, impacting all mankind.

14 Blessings Lost in the Fall of Man

But your iniquities have separated you from your God; And your sins have hidden His face from you, So that He will not hear. – Isaiah 59: 2 (NKJV)

It is intriguing how many spiritual blessings Humanity were lost in the Fall of Adam and Eve. From reading scripture, we have a look into the World that Adam experienced before his temptation by Satan. There are fourteen very significant blessings that we lost by sin entering into this world. 1. Eternal Life (Romans 5: 12-21; Ephesians 2.) 2. Communion with God (Isaiah 59:2.) 3. Fellowship with animals (Genesis 9:2). 4. Control over all aspects of this world (Psalm 8). 5. Freedom from Satan (John 14:30; 2 Corinthian 4:4; Ephesians 6:10-18; Revelation 12:9). 6. God-consciousness (Genesis 2:25; 3:7). 7. The will to always do good (Genesis 6:5-7; Romans 7). 8. Self-Control (Ephesians 2; Galatians 5). 9. Right to the Tree of Life (Genesis 3:22-24). 10. The Garden of Eden (Genesis 2:15; 3:22-24). 11. God's glory (Romans 3:23). 12. Holiness and Righteous (Ephesians 4:22-24). 13. The Blessings of having a perfect union with God (Revelations 21:1-7; 22:1-3). 14. Perfect Health (Genesis 3:16; Matthew 8:17; 1 Peter 2:24).

The original sinless man once had full access to all of these wonderful joyous blessings. Only one man would come after, with the fullness of all these blessings and the ability to keep the Law of Moses perfectly. Jesus did what Adam could not. Christ was able to resist sin and give eternal life unto those who believe in his death, burial and resurrection. Believing in the Lord Jesus Christ not only restores all that was lost in the fall of man, but washes away the genetically inherited sinful nature. According to 1 Corinthians 6:11 (NKJV):

> *And such were some of you. But you were washed, but you were sanctified, but you were justified in the name of the Lord Jesus and by the Spirit of our God.*

Let us now examine some key events that the Gospel directly addresses. These events emphasize the need for a Messiah. They relate to the needs, wants, and cries of humanity since the fall. The Gospel addresses all questions in the Messiah Jesus Christ.

Death, Burial, and Resurrection the Foundation of all Faith

Now if Christ is preached that He has been raised from the dead, how do some among you say that there is no resurrection of the dead, then Christ is not risen. And if Christ is not risen, then our preaching is empty and your faith is also empty. – Apostle Paul in 1 Corinthians 15:12-14 (NKJV)

The basis of our Faith lies in the only way for man to escape his sinful nature and eternal separation from God. This is through Our Faith in the Lord Jesus Christ the Son of God. Having a devoted love for all creation, God humbled Himself and was born a sinless perfect man unto a virgin, to die for the sins of the world. The Lord knew that the only way for sin to be abolished from His creation was in fact to become one Himself. By living a sinless life, Christ was the perfect sacrifice to pay for the sins of the world (since there is no one who is without sin). By going to the cross, Jesus died so that we could live free from the evil desires of our flesh. On the third day, He rose from the dead showing God's approval of His sacrifice for the world. As the scripture states, the power of the resurrection of Christ and our belief in Him frees us from the bondage of sin! This is the Gospel of Jesus Christ. The power of salvation sent from God.

His Sacrifice, was Our gain

But he was wounded for our transgressions, he was bruised for our iniquities: the chastisement of our peace was upon him; and with his stripes we are healed. – Isaiah 53:5 (NKJV)

The above scripture is perhaps one of the most important scriptures found in the Holy Bible. The Prophet Isaiah is speaking about the coming Messiah Jesus Christ and just what He would do for all of Mankind through His death. He is describing just what the wages of Our Sin would do to His mortal body. "He was wounded for Our transgressions," relates to the Cross and just how The Lord would die by Crucifixion. "He was bruised for our iniquities," indicates that what He suffered was not for Himself but for all of Us. "The wages of sin is death (Romans 6:23) which had to be paid for the remission of Sin. "The chastisement of our peace was upon Him," refers to being made right in the eyes of God. Before the Death and Resurrection of Jesus Christ, all of Mankind was in eternal debt to God, who could not dwell with man due to the sinful nature that inhabited His body.

As in the Old Testament of The Holy Bible, the blood shed on altars from animals could not atone for just how deeply sin infected our being. God in His Grace and Mercy sent Christ to die instead, to cover us so that His Holy Spirit could dwell in all who believe by simply placing their Faith in Jesus Christ and Him Crucified. The phrase "And with His stripes we are healed" pertains more to spiritual healing than physical healing. The Messiah's death allows the will of God to operate totally in Our Spirit, Mind and Bodies. Overcoming sin is by no means an easy task. No matter how wealthy or knowledgeable a man is, He can never make himself right by any means other than by the Cross of Jesus Christ. Sin could only be overcome by God Himself, due to the fact that the price was Spiritual and too big for anyone to pay. I take joy in Isaiah 53:5, knowing that God cared enough for me to send His Son Jesus to die, so that we all can be healed.

The Lord Jesus Christ; the Hope for all Humanity

One of the most important aspects of the Christian Faith is to always keep our hope securely placed in the will of God. Through Faith in the Lord Jesus Christ, we are granted the Grace and Mercy of God, and therefore His will for our lives. The Bible states in Psalm 84:11(NKJV), "For the LORD God is a sun and shield: the LORD will give grace and glory: no good thing will he withhold from those who walk uprightly." This pertains to health, perseverance, peace of mind, and overall joy that is in Our Lord Jesus.

In the above scripture "The Lord is my sun and shield" states all that one needs is found in Christ Jesus, namely in the remission of sin in the Believers life. This is due to the presence of the Holy Spirit at work in our lives, who works only within Faith in the Cross of Jesus Christ (Romans 8). By way of the Holy Spirit, the will of God is done in our lives. But we must know that God is in control and that His will for us is perfect. The same way that Jesus prayed the will of the Father in the Garden of Gethsemane in Mark 14:36 (NKJV), "And he said, 'Our, Father, all things are possible for You; take this cup away from me: nevertheless not what I will, but what YOU WILL.'"

All Christians must trust in God, who is omnipotent and knows all as opposed to us and others who do not know just what tomorrow will bring. Being submissive to the will of God is also stated in the Lord's Prayer found in Matthew 6:9-13 (NKJV),

> *In this manner therefore pray: Our Father in heaven, Hallowed be Your name. Your kingdom come, Your will be done on earth, as it is in heaven. Give us this day our daily bread. And forgive us our debts, as we forgive our debtors. And do not lead us into temptation, but deliver us from the evil one. For Yours is the kingdom, and the power, and the glory, forever. Amen.*

The Cross of Christ produces the hope that all will be made right in our lives, no matter what things may look like to us. The Lord's will is manifested in the life of the Believer. As believers we keep our Faith planted at the cross and our hope in the will of God.

Life in the Cross of Christ

Jesus said to him, "I am the way, the truth, and the life. No one comes to the Father except through Me.
– John 14: 6 (NKJV)

While studying the Word of God, it is very important for every student of the Bible to know exactly what the Messiah is saying to His Disciples, both then and now. This is not only important for building our Faith in the Cross of Christ, but also when it comes to ministering to the world and edifying the body of Christ. In John 14:6, Jesus touches on three very important aspects in which all of mankind is redeemed through His perfect sacrifice on the Cross. Jesus states that He is **the way, the truth, and the life** in order to be made right in the eyes of God. We will break down first in **the way** that mankind is made right with God. Mankind is taking on His righteousness and accepting the Messiah as Lord and Savior of our life. All men due to the fall of Adam and Eve are born into sin and shaped in iniquity, separated from God the Father. All when we are birthed into this world have no sense of right or wrong. Men adhere more at times to our flesh rather than the Spirit of God. This thorn in the flesh called sin causes us all to fall short of the Holiness of Jehovah and the original divine plan laid out for us as children of God.

The Holy Bible states that the wages of sin are death (Romans 6:23), which guarantees all eternal separation from God until we accept Jesus Christ as our Savior. Christ is the only one to walk the Earth truly pure and innocent in the eyes of God, never knowing sin. As read in 2 Corinthians 5:21:"For He made Him who knew no sin to be sin for us, that we might become the righteousness of God in Him." Jesus instead took our sins to the cross. 1 Peter 2:24 (NKJV) states: "Who Himself bore our sins in His own body on the tree, that we, having died to sins, might live for righteousness – by whose stripes you were healed." God's word never changes. In His love for us a sacrifice had to be made. Jesus Christ is the only one pure enough to wash away every sin and redeem corrupted man.

The second aspect of John 14:6 is that the Messiah is **the truth** that fulfilled the Old Testament prophecy. Jesus, being born of a virgin, as read in Isaiah 7:14, is fulfilled in Matthew 1:20-23. The Old Testament says that Jesus would be of the House of Judah in Isaiah 37:31 fulfilled in Matthew 1:1-2, 16. Isaiah 9:1-2 says Christ would come from Nazareth of Galilee and documented in Matthew 2:22-23. The betrayal for thirty pieces of silver in

Zechariah 11:12 was fulfilled in Matthew 26:14-15. Along the mission to the Gentiles for salvation as recorded in Isaiah 49:1-4, 6 and fulfilled in Matthew 12:14-21. Lastly, John 14:6 states that Jesus is the life. This quality is always the most often overlooked in a Christian's life. 2 Peter 1:5-9 (NKJV) reads:

> *But also for this very reason, giving all diligence, add to your faith virtue, to virtue knowledge, to knowledge self-control, to self-control perseverance, to perseverance godliness, to godliness brotherly kindness, and to brotherly kindness love. For if these things are yours and abound, you will be neither barren nor unfruitful in the knowledge of our Lord Jesus Christ. For he who lacks these things is shortsighted, even to blindness, and has forgotten that he was cleansed from his old sins.*

The above list includes moral attributes to govern our lives by that all in the Faith of Jesus Christ must allow to overflow in our lives, along with *forgiveness*. Once we realize the debt we could not pay, but He who could (the way) and (the truth) He who came, and how to live our lives (the life), we will finally see God the Father.

Jesus Christ: The great "I AM"

Jesus said to them, "Most assuredly, I say to you, before Abraham was, I AM. – John 8:58 (NKJV), "

One of the most important doctrines of the Christian faith is the belief that Jesus Christ was the Son of God, and that His only begotten Son died for all Humanity. In the coming times, many will try to distort the truth of the deity of Christ by saying He was not truly God but only a man who brought knowledge into the world regarding how to live a satisfying life unto God (YAH) and nothing more.

The Bible is clear on the matter of who Christ was, as well as the words spoken by Jesus Himself stating that He is indeed the great I AM.

This phrase refers back to the book of Exodus chapter 3:14 (NKJV) in which God spoke to Moses stating, "And God said to Moses, "I AM WHO I AM." And He said, "Thus you shall say to the children of Israel, "I AM has sent me to you.""

I AM meaning YAHOVEH, or YAH for short, the self-existent living God. Jesus used this same statement several times in the Gospel of John. The first is John 6:35 (NKJV) (as well as verses 41, 48, 51, of the same chapter): "And Jesus said to them, "I AM the bread of life. He who comes to Me shall never hunger, and he who believes in Me shall never thirst." Here the Messiah is letting His followers know He and the Father are one in nature and the believer has everything they will need in Him. John 8: 12 (NKJV) reads: "Then Jesus spoke to them again, saying, "I

AM the light of the world. He who follows Me shall not walk in darkness, but have the light of life." Once again Christ is referring to YAH and Himself as one, bringing light unto the world. In John 10:7, 9 (NKJV) Jesus states, "Then Jesus said to them again, "Most assuredly, I say to you, I AM the door of the sheep." This lets us know that He is a protector to His sheep (us) from the trials of this world. John 10:11, 14 supports the same claim of Jesus as the protector from those who are in Him from all harm of this world. In John 11:25 (NKJV), Jesus said to her, "I AM the resurrection and the life. He who believes in Me, though he may die, he shall live." Christ professes eternal life for those who believe in Him, granted by the living God (YAH) who raised the Messiah from the dead to show His sacrifice was good in His eyes for the sins of the world. In John 14: 6 (NKJV), "Jesus said to him, 'I AM the way, the truth, and the life. No one comes to the Father except through Me.'" This lets all know that He is all truth and knowledge of the living God for those spiritually dead. Jesus Christ is the only one able to keep the Old Testament law to please the Father, and offer up Himself as a perfect sacrifice for our sins. This is why all humanity must receive Christ and repent. In John 15:1, (NKJV) the Messiah states: "I AM the true vine, and My Father is the vinedresser." In the Old Testament, it is stated many times that Israel is YAH's true vine, but due to their idolatry and unfaithfulness never bore fruit for the living God. In Jesus Christ's return, He will reclaim what Israel and Humanity lost in the fall. Jesus the son is the Father, and the Father is the son, in the same essence and substance. I pray none of us forgets these scriptures and that we grow in knowledge of Jesus Christ, the great I AM.

Eli, Eli, Lama Sabachthani

And about the ninth hour Jesus cried out with a loud voice, saying, Eli, Eli, lama sabachthani? that is, My God, My God, why have You forsaken me? – Matthew 27:46 (NKJV)

"Eli, Eli Lama Sabachthani" was a very prophetic statement uttered by Yeshua/Jesus Christ as He suffered for sins on the Cross. Here Jesus is confirming His death as the final sin, offering for all mankind by quoting a passage from Psalm 22:1-3 (NKJV). This passage states, "My God, my God, why You forsaken me? Why are You so far from helping Me, and from the words of my groaning? O my God, I cry in the day time, but You do not hear, and in the night season, and am not silent. But You are holy, Enthroned in the praises of Israel."

This scripture, written by King David many years prior to the Lord's arrival here on Earth, stated that in His time of need David looked to the Cross of Christ and the Messiah as refuges from suffering and hardship here on Earth. Christ spoke these same words from the Cross, which laid claim to Jesus Christ as the Lamb of God and the only true salvation for all of mankind for the remission of all sin. Every Disciple of Christ should diligently seek the Lord and look to the Cross as our only means of salvation, the same way King David did when He had too much to bare.

No amount of good deeds can replace the fact that the Cross of Christ is truly one's only help in times of need. It is only by way of Yeshua/Jesus Christ that the Holy Spirit can intercede on our behalf, having our Faith placed correctly in the Cross. Then and only then can we be delivered from this world, as stated in Psalm 22: 4-5 (NKJV): "Our fathers trusted in You; They trusted, and You delivered them. They cried to You, and were delivered: They trusted in You, and were not ashamed."

The Preeminence of Jesus Christ

"For you died, and your life is hidden with Christ in God."
– Colossians 3:3 (NKJV),

The glory of the Lord is displayed in every major aspect of our being today. The Most High God has embedded the superiority of Christ and our need for repentance as the means to achieve our purpose in Him. Through the covenant of the New Testament, God implanted a sure way to be made right and whole in His eyes. This can only happen through the acceptance of Jesus. Christ is the rock of this foundation, and most importantly in the reconciliation unto God His resurrection made. Colossians 1:21-22 (NKJV) reads: "And you, who once were alienated and enemies in your mind by wicked works, yet now He has reconciled in the body of His flesh through death, to present you holy, and blameless, and above reproach in His sight."

Many people forget that there is still only one true way to please God, and that is through Christ atonement at the Cross. There is no other means. The Most High calls on those who have ears to hear into repentance through Christ and the perfect sacrifice He made. The Bible states that Jesus is the light of the world (John 8:12), and this light is visible to all those who have eyes to see. This light is namely visible in government, in the election of a leader to guide and uphold the righteousness of the people for a higher quality of life. A president or governor is a representation of a type of Christ, working for the people of a nation. Many forms of governmental power foreshadow the need for a perfect powerful leader, which when compared to Jesus, holds no resemblance. Colossians 1:17 (NKJV): "And He is before all things, and in Him all things consist." Jesus is everything every man or woman would need based on of His duality with God.

In our hunger to eat, the teachings of Jesus Christ are present in His statement of being the "Bread of Life"(John 6:48). This is evident in the way we need food at times, indicating our spirituality is also in dire need. The daily work ethic of waking up is symbolic of the spiritual struggle of working toward the goals of the Most High, present in our fall from grace, in which God cursed Adam. Genesis 3:22-23 (NKJV) reads: "Then the Lord God said, 'Behold, the man has become like one of Us, to know good and evil. And now, lest he put out his hand and take also of the tree of life, and eat, and live forever.' Therefore, the Lord God sent him out of the garden of Eden to till the ground from which he was taken."

The work we all put in on a weekly basis is based of the original sin of Adam. This reminds of our need for a Savior. The preeminence of Christ is focused most strongly on our own humanity, in our imperfections and bad desires. Colossians 3:5-14 (NKJV) states:

Therefore, put to death your members which are on the Earth: fornication, uncleanness, passion, evil desire, and covetousness, which is idolatry. Because of these things the wrath of God is coming upon the sons of disobedience, in which you yourselves once walked when you lived in them. But now you yourselves are to put off all these: anger, wrath, malice, blasphemy, filthy language out of your mouth. Do not lie to one another, since you have put off the old man with his deeds, and have put on the new man who is renewed in knowledge according to the image of Him who created him, where there is neither Greek nor Jew, circumcised nor uncircumcised, barbarian, Scythian, slave nor free, but Christ is all and in all.

In the times that we as human beings fall short, we are reminded of one who never did, and who has come to redeem us. Through the sacrifice of the son Jesus we all get a chance to see the Father. Consider this a friendly reminder is that all roads do not lead to God, but if you look close all roads lead to Christ.

The Blood of Jesus Christ

But if we walk in the light, as he is in the light, we have fellowship with one another, and the blood of Jesus Christ his Son cleanses us from all sin. – 1 John 1:7 (NKJV)

Blood as defined in the English dictionary is "a specialized bodily fluid that delivers necessary substance (oxygen, nutrients) to the body's cell, while transporting waste product away from those very same cells in."

YAH, the living God, is very well adapted to teaching His children spiritual occurrences through natural means for our own understanding. In this case, the Holy Spirit uses the bodily functions of human blood to explain the Spiritual ramifications of Christ's own bloodshed on Calvary 2,000 years ago. The Blood of Christ did more than simply do away with the Old Testament sacrificial system. Just like the blood that runs through our own veins, the Lord's blood carries the necessary spiritually for all who believe in Him to live a victorious life while we remain in the flesh, awaiting His return. The Word of God defines those in Christ as a body as read in 1 Corinthians 12:12 (NKJV): "For as the body is one and has many members, but all the members of that one body, being many, are one body, so also is Christ."

As a collective we function as such, in the spreading of the Gospel of Christ with his blood carrying the much needed substance to all just like our own natural blood. Jesus' blood carries three crucial nutrients to those who have accepted Jesus. The first is forgiveness throughout the

Body of Christ, as read in Revelations 1:5 (NKJV): "And from Jesus Christ, the faithful witness, the firstborn from the dead, and the ruler over the kings of the earth. To Him who loved us and washed us from our sins in His own blood." In knowing that we are sinful and rely on the precious Blood of Jesus, our sins past, present, and future are cleansed.

The second important nutrient is total victory! Christ's blood gives us the power to overcome the powers of the enemy and the schemes laid before us. Revelations 12:11 (NKJV) states, "And they overcame him by the blood of the Lamb and by the word of their testimony; and they did not love their lives to the death." The Lord will never leave or forsake any of His own in our time of need. Any and everything is given unto Us to overcome through our Faith in the Cross and what Jesus did on it. Much of what we endure is according to the will God in each season, to perfect our Faith as needed. Trials are to glorify the

Father and promote Jesus Christ as His son. There is no better testimony than that of someone who overcomes through the Blood of Jesus. The third function of the Blood of Christ to the body is sanctification (or being one with the Lord). Hebrews 10:10 (NKJV) says: "By that will we have been sanctified through the offering of the body of Jesus Christ once for all." In knowing Jesus, we become one with Him, having His strength and right relationship with God. The Blood is total victory for the Body of Christ and all who truly know Him. I pray that we all come together as one body and allow the Blood of Jesus to Forgive, Sanctify, and grant all total victory in Christ.

It Is Finished

So when Jesus had received the sour wine, he said, "It is finished!" and bowing His head, He gave up His spirit. – John 19:30 (NKJV)

The greatest words ever uttered in Human history came from our Lord Jesus Christ by simply saying, "it is finished." With only these three words the sin debt brought into Humanity by Adam and Eve was paid in full by way of the Cross of Christ. The imperfect man was granted Grace and Mercy with Forgiveness, which is a gift to all who would accept the Gospel of Jesus Christ. This is only after accepting that Jesus has taken away the sins that every man and woman commits. Jesus paid the highest price for our sins not simply through his words. He also did so through the fulfillment of the Law of Moses, which is the high standard of perfection that God called for everyone to follow and obey. Since Jesus was both God and Man, He was the only one pure enough to hold true to every law passed down to Moses, as stated in the book of Exodus Chap 20:1-17. The Sabbath was kept Holy, the day of rest can now be found in Jesus Christ Matthew 11:28 (NKJV). "Come to Me, all you who labor and are heavy laden, and I will give you rest." By placing one's Faith in the finished work at the Cross the Lord can become free all from any heartache stated in Galatians 5:1-6 (NKJV):

> *Stand fast, therefore in the liberty by which Christ has made us free, and do not be entangled again with a yoke of bondage. Indeed I, Paul, say to you that if you become circumcised, Christ will profit you nothing. And I testify again to every man who becomes circumcised that he is a debtor to keep the whole law. You have become estranged from Christ, you who attempt to be justified by law; you have fallen from grace. For we through the Spirit eagerly wait for the hope of righteousness by faith. For in Christ Jesus neither circumcision nor uncircumcision avails anything, but faith working through love.*

We are secured by being placed in the Divine will of God, with His will being nothing short of being truly blessed by Him through Jesus Christ. Sickness cannot remain, depression must bow out, and sin cannot abound in the presence of God! Let those who are suffering from sin be relieved of their burden because Christ has taken it for them on the Cross. By simply believing on the Cross, Jesus will tell them at last: "It is finished."

The Omnipresence of God

Where can I go from Your spirit? Or where can I flee from Your presence? If I ascend up into heaven, You are there; if I make my bed in hell, behold, You are there. If I take the wings of the morning, and dwell in the uttermost parts of the sea; Even there Your hand shall lead me, and Your right hand shall hold me. – Psalm 139:7-10 (NKJV),

The word *omnipresence* is defined as being present in every place at the same time; unbounded or having universal presence. The omnipresence of God is one of the divine characteristics of our Lord, in which many believers in the Faith should study and apply in their lives. Knowing that God almighty is in control of every situation we endure is a comforting fact. It is a great Faith-builder as a Disciple of Jesus Christ. At times as believers, we have the tendency to believe that God (YAH) is not with us when things do not go our way or turn out the way we want. In fact, He is the author and the finisher of all things in the lives of those who believe in Him, whether good or bad. God is the ultimate craftsman! This is in knowing what each and every characteristic His children need to develop or be strengthened in. Proverbs 15:3 (NKJV) states: "The eyes of the LORD are in every place, keeping watch on the evil and the good."

With God being present in Heaven and in the Earth as we know Deuteronomy 4:39 (NKJV): "Therefore know this day, and consider it in your heart, that the LORD Himself is God in heaven above, and on the earth beneath: there is no other." With God being ever present in our lives, we need to look for Him and seek every opportunity to build up our spirituality to know more of Him. In some cases, this may be the result of dealing with a death in the family, sickness, or a difficult co-worker. You see, God knew beforehand that this situation would arise; He is ever-present! The Lord looks for us to deal with the ills of this world and grow in Faith, just as Christ did. God may even cause Satan described in the Bible as our footstool (Romans 16:19-20) to cause disruption for us like the Lord allowed in the Book of Job. The central idea is to let all those who believe know that God is in control of our lives. We have no purpose other than what He ordains for us to be. This gives many the freedoms to live out His will and not our own. Job 2:10 (NKJV) states: "But he said to her, 'You speak as one of the foolish women speaks. Shall we indeed accept good from God, and shall we not accept adversity? In all this Job did not sin with his lips.'"

God uses the enemy at many ways to produce love, patience, kindness, virtue and moral excellence in His children, by allowing hardship and temptation in our lives. He knows that by resisting we grow closer to Jesus Christ. The next time someone wrongs you, or your health is taken for a season, remember that God is present and will see you through it. God will always keep you always in His presence.

Come All unto Christ, and He Will Give You Rest

Come unto me, all you who labor and are heavy laden, and I will give you rest. Take my yoke upon you, and learn from me; for I am gentle and lowly in heart: and you will find rest for your souls. For my yoke is easy, and My burden is light. – Matthew 11:28-30 (NKJV)

It is an extreme blessing to know that Jesus Christ is not so different from us; that in times of need He can comfort us in all our trials and tribulations. The scripture above lays the foundation of the Christian Faith by Our Lord, if we read between the lines. Christ states "Come unto me", in which Jesus reveals that He is the only way to Salvation and to be made right in the eyes of God. "All ye who labor and are heavy laden" refers to those unsaved who are trying to find comfort in anything other than Jesus Christ and His perfect sacrifice, only to be met with heartache and rejection. "I will give you rest" speaks of the access unto Salvation and favor by God, placing one's Faith in His perfect sacrifice. "Take My yoke upon you", represents the denial of your own will power to be in total submission unto God (Luke 9:23).

Then Jesus states, "And learn of Me". This process is learning of just what the Crucifixion means to the Believer. This can be read in (Romans 6:3-5). "For I am meek and lowly in heart". In this passage, Jesus says that He is all-understanding in each and every situation. "And ye shall find rest unto your souls". This rest can come only by Faith in Christ and His perfect sacrifice for all sin. "For my yoke is easy, and My burden is light" is the Messiah stating that there is little required of us except that we believe. We can do this by simply placing our Faith in the Cross of Christ. We accept Faith that our sins have been paid for and that we no longer are held captive by them. This is all that is needed. Truly believing that you are now dead to sin and that the Cross affects your life in every way for the good is the true rest that mankind needs.

Jesus the Willing Messiah

Now a leper came to Him, imploring Him, kneeling down to Him and saying to Him, 'If You are willing, You can make me clean.' Then Jesus, moved with compassion, stretched out His hand and touched him, and said to him, 'I am willing; be cleansed.' As soon as He had spoken, immediately the leprosy left him, and he was cleansed. – Mark 1:40-42 (NKJV)

A good testimony of the will of the Father is that He is willing to meet His children in every walk of life in order to give them salvation. Mark 1:40-42 speaks of a man stricken with leprosy and seeking healing from the

Messiah. This story is also symbolic of many who suffer and struggle with the sinful nature we all are born into. God is not so far off that He does not know we are in desperate need to be aligned to His will. The Father knows the heart of each and every one of us and in His generosity. He offers us sinless protection in Jesus Christ. No matter what walk of life, no matter what sin is currently binding us and drawing us away from God, the scripture says He has compassion for us as we are in turmoil. Salvation is for all at any moment. Ephesians 1:3-8 (NKJV) states:

> *Blessed be the God and Father of our Lord Jesus Christ, who has blessed us with every spiritual blessing in the heavenly places in Christ, just as He chose us in Him before the foundation of the world, that we should be holy and without blame before Him in love, having predestined us to adoption as sons by Jesus Christ to Himself, according to the good*

pleasure of His will, to the praise of the glory of His grace, by which He made us accepted in the Beloved. In Him we have redemption through His blood, the forgiveness of sins, according to the riches of His grace which He made to abound toward us in all wisdom and prudence.

It is God's good pleasure that we be holy and blameless in His eyes. This is according for us as Children of God to see and ask for a change in our life through His will. Revelations 3:20 (NKJV) reads: "Behold, I stand at the door and knock. If anyone hears My voice and opens the door, I will come in to him and dine with him, and he with Me." It doesn't matter where we are in life or how far we think we are from the Lord. The Messiah is always willing if we ask that He enters our life and makes us whole. Many of us have been abandoned by loved ones, addicted to narcotics, and indulged in lustful desires. But

God is still here for us if we choose to believe in the son Jesus Christ. I always remember Ezekiel 16:6 (NKJV) where the Prophet records the love of God for Jerusalem who were given into much sin.

And when I passed by you and saw you struggling in your own blood, I said to you in your blood, "Live!" Yes, I said to you in your blood, "Live!" God is saying the same to Us today, as a people who struggle with sin and our true identity in this world. Can we look to Him and ask "Lord are you willing," and the answer is always "Yes!"

Chosen, blessed, broken and redeemed through Christ

For there were about 5,000 men. Then He said to His disciples, "Make them sit down in groups of fifty." And they did so, and made them all sit down.

Then He took the five loaves and the two fish, and looking up to heaven, He blessed and broke them, and gave them to the disciples to set before the multitude. So they all ate and were filled, and twelve baskets of the leftover fragments were taken up by them. – Luke 9:14-17

Many Christian Disciples pray for the redemption process that God has set in motion for those chosen for His glory. Once we are saved by the blood Jesus Christ shed for our sins, the purification process has begun. This commences the shifting of our souls to see what is pleasing to God and what is not. Luke 9:14-17 provides us a very good example of just what the Lord does. He receives us, blesses us, and breaks us of the way we think, act, and say. Only then can we truly testify on His behalf for all He has done for us. We have a tendency to look past this part though, only wishing to get the blessings that God has. But the Lord needs us to be rebuilt before we can be positioned to do His work. This means that some places that you used to enjoy going to will now be off limits, because it doesn't line up with Him. Some friendships may end because old friends can give birth to old sins. Remember Amos 3:3 (NKJV): "Can two walk together, unless they are agreed?"

From time to time we are going to bump heads with the old man after being born again. Just know that something better is awaiting you on the other side once we are glorified in Christ! The breaking and mending back together is all for the glory of God the Father who in grace and mercy chose you to receive the gift of Jesus Christ.

The Grace and Mercy of the Lord Jesus Christ

Seeing then that we have a great High Priest who has passed through the heavens, Jesus the Son of God, let us hold fast our confession. For we do not have a High Priest who cannot sympathize with our weaknesses, but was in all points tempted as we are, yet without sin. Let us therefore come boldly to the throne of grace, that we may obtain mercy and find grace to help in time of need. – . Hebrews 4:14-16 (NKJV)

Grace in Christianity is defined as unmerited divine favor on the behalf of God. This gift comes to those who are repentant of their sins and accept the sacrifice of the Lord Jesus Christ for the remission of sin that exists in every man and woman created. Grace comes solely based on the fact that we, as children of the Most High, are not perfect creatures as we were originally created to be. This also comes from God, who knows that sinful man cannot live a perfect life according to His will. The Lord knows this based on the Son Jesus Christ, who walked among mankind for over thirty years, feeling the same temptation that we feel in these mortal bodies. Jesus was tempted by Satan in Luke 4:1-13 but never sinned, due to the fact no sinful nature was present in him due to his divine nature. This makes mercy readily available to those who ask for it. The Lord knows how each and every person was born in sin and shaped in iniquity. He knows we had no choice when we came into this sinful, fallen world. In Christ's perfect mercy, He gives His power to Us who believe. The power to overcome Luke 10:19 (NKJV) reads: "Behold, I give you the authority to trample on serpents and scorpions, and over all the power of the enemy, and nothing shall by any means hurt you."

Jesus says here that no Spiritual infirmity will come our way that we do not have the power to overcome in His name. This includes Satan, Fallen Angels, and Demonic Spirits that influence Earthly matters in order to steal, kill and destroy. This Divine power is the same Jesus Christ used to resist the Devil and heal the sick. But more importantly, this includes submission to the Will of God, which is the ultimate goal for every Christian. At times when we fail the Lord and fall short of His standard of Holiness, it is important to know that His mercy sustains us. Jesus knows the difficult task we have in this life and grants those who believe the Grace to make mistakes. He also grants us the power to overcome them. God is omnipresent in all of our situations, and hardship comes to perfect the Saints for the Lord's purpose. In short, Grace is the ability to be forgiven and the Mercy of the Lord is to overcome.

Jesus calms the storm

On the same day, when evening had come, He said to them, "Let us cross over to the other side." Now when they had left the multitude, they took Him along in the boat as He was. And other little boats were also with Him. And a great windstorm arose, and the waves beat into the boat, so that it was already filling. But He was in the stern, asleep on a pillow. And they awoke Him and said to Him, "Teacher, do You not care that we are perishing?" Then He arose and rebuked the wind, and said to the sea, "Peace, be still!" And the wind ceased and there was a great calm. But He said to them, "Why are you so fearful? How is it that you have no faith?" And they feared exceedingly, and said to one another, "Who can this be, that even the wind and the sea obey Him!" - Mark 4: 35-41(NKJV)

Mark 4:35-41 provides a remarkable account of being a servant unto the will of God. The Gospel of Mark gives believers a description of Jesus Christ as God's servant continually doing the Father's will while here on Earth. The above scriptures describe an event after a day of teaching many people from different walks of life of the Kingdom of God. Jesus gives His Disciples the instruction for them, to "cross over unto the other side of the waters," in which a storm arose while Jesus was asleep. This storm is symbolic of the trials many Christians face as we await the second return of the Messiah. It is important to remember that as long as we stay consecrated to the Word of God we have no fear as to what this life may bring. The Disciples lost Faith that the Lord instructed them to "cross over the water" in which then the storm arose. We know that as long as we follow the Christ, we will never be in danger. This is because in Christ we are secure. This is stated in Hebrews 13:6 (NKJV):

So we may boldly say: "The Lord is my helper; I will not fear. What can man do to me." Jesus Christ is never wrong when He gives instructions unto His followers! If we are met with opposition, (which is always a plan of the enemy 1 Peter 5:8) trust in the Word of God to always see you through.

Psalm 40:1-3 (NKJV) states:

I waited patiently for the Lord; and He inclined to me, and heard my cry. He also brought me up also out of a horrible pit, out of the miry clay, and set my feet upon a rock, and established my steps. And He has put a new song in my mouth- Praise unto our God: Many will see it, and fear, And trust in the Lord.

Faith in the Cross of Christ

Jesus said to him, "If you can believe, all things are possible to him who believes. – Mark 9:23 (NKJV)

Throughout His Earthly ministry, Jesus often expressed that all things are possible to those who believed in the finished work of the Cross. The work that Christ proclaimed was finished in John 19:30 was the freeing of mankind from the sin debt that impaired the ability of humans to function as a true child of God. Jesus took away the dominion of sin, and in return let us be the master over sin instead of a slave to it (Romans 6:14). By placing our Faith in the Cross, the true believer of the Gospel can receive this revelation from God by simply believing that "It is finished." This allows the Holy Spirit to function within the life of all Christians (John 14:26).

Our Faith frees us from the bondage of sin, but we are still to be perfected by it in order to fully grow into the image of Christ. This means that the problems of the world should not worry us so much, because the Messiah overcame it already at Calvary. The debt has been paid! So in return we can simply ask the Holy Spirit to guide us and comfort us through this fallen world and to glorify us in the end. With the high price of sin paid ,the Biblical scriptures act as receipts for Christ's sacrifice on our behalf. This is why when Believers become disenchanted, we can remember Proverbs 15:18 or Psalm 4:4. In extreme challenges, I like to recite Joshua 1:5. In times of depression, I often read Psalm 55:22, Philippians 4:6-7, Jonah 2:2, and Psalm 9:9. The Holy Bible always reinstates if only we believe that all things are possible.

and confirmed That I will keep Your righteous judgments. I am afflicted very much; Revive me, O Lord, according to Your word. Accept, I pray, the freewill offerings of my mouth, O Lord, And teach me Your judgments.

This descriptive detail of Jesus is the very same way all believers are to order their lives as Disciples of Christ! We should not enjoy the company of ungodly nonbelievers but follow the path of the righteous in order to be fed spiritually and edify others in the body of Christ. There is much joy in reading the scriptures of the Most High and meditating on them so we too can live a prosperous life in the Lord. This proper meditation on each verse of the Holy Bible will plant us safely by the rivers of water (Holy Spirit) to bring forth fruit in due season. We will not wither away but lead prosperous lives for the Christ. Psalm 1:1-3 speaks of life not only here in the natural world, but most importantly of the second coming of Jesus. We enjoy our time here, but always yearn for that precious day in which we will hear "well done". I pray all will take the time to mold himself in the way of Jesus Christ as He walked here while on the Earth, being the perfect role model for humanity.

Presenting Ourselves as a Living Sacrifice for Christ

I beseech you therefore, brethren, by the mercies of God, that you present your bodies a living sacrifice, holy, acceptable to God, which is your reasonable service. And do not be conformed to this world, but be transformed by the renewing of your mind, that you may prove what is that good and acceptable and perfect will of God. – Romans 12:1-2 (NKJV)

The term "a living sacrifice" has become misconstrued in today's Christian world, where the godly and ungodly are beginning to intermingle. In our repentance from sin and turn toward Christ for new life, we sometimes forget just what exactly we are being held accountable for in this new walk. The Bible states in Colossians 3:3 (NKJV), "For you died, and your life is hidden with Christ in God." In the same way that Jesus died for our sins, we are to die to the needs and the wants of our old self. In Jesus we are to begin thinking with a new mindset; one totally focused on having a godly perspective. This means not partaking in the part of this world in which sin is growing more prevalent and inevitable. Instead of the world, we should showcase the Gospel of salvation and just how belief in the Messiah can transform everyone's life to begin anew. In the Holy Bible, the term "holy" means to be set apart, different from everyone else to showcase the Christ nature to the unsaved" (Romans 12:1-2). This is preemptively displayed through grace and mercy. We were sinners at some time in our lives, and the light of God was shown to us. It called us out of the darkness of this world. In displaying these characteristics, it makes us acceptable unto God and enables the Holy Spirit to flow to many for the repentance from sin.

As a living sacrifice we complete the good news of the departed Savior. We spread the Gospel of Jesus Christ to the four corners of the world to prompt the return of the Messiah. "And this gospel of the kingdom will be preached the world over as a witness to all the nations. And then the end will come" Matthew 24:14 (NKJV). Through the Assembly of the Saints, we set the example and preach the good news of Christ sacrifice. We allow the Kingdom of God to be shown through us and one day usher in the return of the anointed Savior Jesus Christ.

Love the Lord, and keep His Commandments

If you love Me, keep My commandments. And I will pray the Father, and He will give you another Helper, that He may abide with you forever. – John 14:15-16 (NKJV)

An important message given to man by the Messiah is that of keeping the original Law of Moses, as told in Exodus 20:1-17. Many think today that all we have to do is believe in Christ, and prosperity, miracles and blessings will flow with abundance in our life. To our Faith, we must also add the original Law as handed down to Moses from God, the Ten Commandments. God commanded man to:

1) Have no other gods before me. This is the number one law. Unfortunately, many people do not keep it. Instead, many pay homage to celebrities, athletes or Pastors before God the Father, without knowing what they are doing. Christians must seek God *first* every day, before

sports, news, celebrity gossip, or our own desires. We must always keep a godly mindset before all things.

2) Worship of Graven Images. THis plays a major part in the world today, especially with items like cellphones, iPads, game systems, and other items in popular culture. I know many people feel totally lost without their cell phone, but never feel that way when they forget to pray to the Father. God is the only one we need to be in constant communication with to follow His Law.

3) Not taking the Lord's name in vain. This has become second nature to many, due to an acceptance of loose morals in today's society. The name of the Lord is still to be revered as YAH THE MOST HIGH, the great "I am."

4) The Sabbath. This has become misconstrued in American Society by changing the day to Sunday instead of

Saturday as God originally intended. Man does not have the right to change the mind of God but to follow His Word.

5) Honoring our Parents. We as a society no longer follow this commandment, because many parents do not hold their parental rights in such high regard as in the past, instead choosing to be "yes" men and women to our children's desires. Disciplining the youth of today is still the right tool for our youth to follow the Law of God. Broken homes also add to the lack of respect in today's youth for parents. When a father or mother is not guiding a child on the right path together as one, the Enemy has successfully destroyed the original image of man that God created.

6) Murder is still a crime against God unless in self-defense of oneself (Exodus 22:2).

7. Thou shall not commit adultery. In the sex-filled world of entertainment, the sinful man or woman will find it very hard to resist temptation as it relates to the flesh.

8) Thou shall not steal. This pertains to even the smallest of items that many Believers commit due to human nature. The "sampling" of fruit at a grocery store or taking items from an office is all stealing inadvertently.

9) Thou shall not bear false witness against thy neighbor. This includes lying or slandering someone we know in order to discredit them. This can always be seen in courtrooms, in which many good people argue about the wrongdoings of someone who is paying them.

10) Covetousness of thy neighbor's goods. Many Believers desire what is not theirs, but which belong to their neighbors. This can include money, cars, a house, and even a wife or husband. All are grave sins in the eyes of God.

The above infractions show that, even today, many Christians still transgress the Law of God. We must remain loyal to the Commandments in order to be made right in the eyes of God. This includes being born again through Christ Jesus, who is the only One who kept the Law of the Most High. Once we accept Jesus, God's Holy Spirit will keep us within the Ten Commandments and in His perfect will (Romans 8).

The most important for all is the law of love given by Jesus in John 13:34-35. "A new commandment I give unto you, that ye love one another; as I have loved you, that ye also love one another. By this shall all men know that ye are my disciples, if ye love one another.

Sanctified to the Lord Jesus Christ

For it is sanctified by the word of God and prayer. – 1 Timothy 4:5 (NJKV)

Sanctification is defined as being set apart for sacred use; to make holy or purify. The Holy Bible strongly promotes sanctification or consecration to the Word of God throughout the scriptures as a means of giving Christians the insight into the mind of God and His true purpose for your life. Constantly having the Lord on your mind and obeying exactly as the Bible states will free us from the confines of this natural world and into the true Kingdom of God. This is imperative in a time when the things of the world will tell us everything is negative in the sense of the economy, physical health, and personal security. Refer to the Holy Scriptures in these dark times! Believe that God can and has set apart those who truly believe, blessing them for their faithfulness.

As stated in Deuteronomy 2:7 (NKJV): "For the Lord your God has blessed you in all the work of your hand. He knows your trudging through this great wilderness. These forty years the Lord your God has been with you; you have lacked nothing." Never allow the enemy to tell you what your life will be! Base all your faith on the fact that God always looks out for His children. This is true in good and bad times. The natural world has no jurisdiction on a supernatural God. Jesus preached this message in Luke 21:34-36 (NKJV):

> *But take heed to yourselves, lest your hearts be weighed down with carousing, drunkenness, and cares of this life, and that Day come on you unexpectedly. For it will come as a snare on all those who dwell on the face of the whole earth. Watch therefore, and pray always that you may be counted worthy to escape all these things that will come to pass, and to stand before the Son of Man.*

This teaching is why we hold onto the Word of God. The more we believe and strengthen our Faith – based on what God says and not what the world says – the stronger we become. In this way, we begin to see His true plan for our lives. The Holy Bible states in John 1:12 (NKJV): "But as many as received Him, to them gave He gave the right to become children of God, to those who believe in his Name."

The Lord knows our needs based on Hebrews 4:14-16 (NKJV):

Seeing then that we have a great High Priest who has passed through the heavens, Jesus the Son of God, let us hold fast our confession. For we do not have a High Priest who cannot sympathize with our weaknesses, but was in all points tempted as we are, yet without sin. Let us therefore come boldly to the throne of grace, that we may obtain mercy and find grace to help in time of need.

Lastly Romans 8:1(NKJV) states: "There is therefore now no condemnation to those who are in Christ Jesus, who do not walk according to the flesh, but according to the Spirit." I pray for more and more strong Brothers and Sisters of the Faith to follow not the news of this world, but the Good News of the Gospel of Jesus Christ. I pray that more strong Brothers and Sisters commit to sanctifying themselves to His Godly attributes through the Holy Bible!

Cleansing Your Temple for Christ

Then He went into the temple and began to drive out those who bought and sold in it, 46 saying to them, It is written, 'My house is a house of prayer,' but you have made it a den of thieves. – Luke 19:45-46 (NKJV)

Luke 19 describes the Jewish Temple in Jerusalem, where observant Jews would offer sacrifices unto God and have fellowship with their kinfolk. Along the road as with many of God's creations, laws, and moral standards, the Temple gradually became corrupt. It basically became a place of business instead of worship. Upon seeing with His own eyes the corruption in the Holy place, Christ drove out all who were partaking in such blasphemous doings. With the death of Jesus on the Cross, and by offering Himself as the perfect sacrifice, Christ transferred the old Temple used for sacrifices to our mortal bodies. Apostle Paul in 1 Corinthians 3:16 states: "Don't you know that you yourselves are God's temple and that God's Spirit lives in you?"

There is no longer a need for sacrifice when the Lord has already died for everyone's sin. And with that we are the living Temple of God, who are to keep our Spirit, Soul, and Body just as pure as the old Jewish Temple. This means the purging of immoral thoughts, acts, and abuse with anything that is ungodly and not of Jesus the Christ, who died so that our salvation may be made easier to please God. Today I pray that we all take a look at ourselves and see what we are thinking about and doing. This includes our intentions toward one another to see if they please God. We may have to purge ourselves, just as Christ did the Temple years ago, through prayer and the renewal of our minds.

To Live as Christ

For to me to live is Christ, and to die is gain. – Philippians 1:21 (NKJV)

In the scripture above, the Apostle Paul spoke about the concept of truly living for the Lord Jesus Christ. The act of complete self-denial of everything that He was to become was that which God truly wants for all of us; to be like Him! Living as Christ is having a total dependency on the will of God. Jesus Christ exhibited this especially during His Earthly ministry, which was spent spreading the good news of the Gospel that was unfolding before their eyes to witness. That God so loved the world that He gave His only son Jesus to die for the sins of the world (John 3:16). There is no greater duty for all Christians while we are here on Earth than to tell everyone what Jesus Christ has done for us through His death, burial and resurrection. The term "die" in Philippians 1:21 refers not to a physical death, but that of our own will. It calls for us to deny our personal beliefs and wants to be more like Him; the same way that Jesus bent His will to that of God. In Matthew 26:39, "He went a little farther, and fell on his face, and prayed, saying, 'O my Father, if it be possible, let this cup pass from me: nevertheless not as I will, but as thou wilt.'"

At the same time, God knows the greater good for our lives and the impact that we will make for His Kingdom on Earth. The "gain," refers to eternal life with

Him. Revelation 21:4 states: "God shall wipe away all tears from their eyes; and there shall be no more death, neither sorrow, nor crying, neither shall there be any more pain: for the former things are passed away." Amen, for the "gain" is eternal peace and security with the Love of God abounding forever with us. It is time to help spread the Gospel of Jesus Christ to someone who doesn't know that Christ has already died so that we don't have to. Be Blessed…

Justification by Faith

Therefore, having been justified by faith, we have peace with God through our Lord Jesus Christ, through whom also we have access by faith into this grace in which we stand, and rejoice in hope of the glory of God. – Romans 5:1-2 (NKJV)

The Greek word for *justification* according to the New Testament of The Holy Bible is *dikaioo*. This word means "to acquit" or "to vindicate" according to the Word of God. This describes the Faith that Christians place in the Lord Jesus as atonement for the "sinful nature" that was inherited by all Mankind from Adam and Eve. This makes all who accept Christ right in the eyes of the one true God. This is made possible only through the Divine Nature of Jesus, being both God and Man who knew no sin. In 2 Corinthians 5:21, we learn that God took the burden of sin, for all of Us to the Cross to be sacrificed on Our behalf. The New Testament states that by Faith we are placed inside His death Spiritually in Romans 6:3-5 stating:

> *Know ye not, that so many of us as were baptized into Jesus Christ were baptized into his death? Therefore we are buried with him by baptism into death: that like as Christ was raised up from the dead by the glory of the Father, even so we also should walk in newness of life. For if we have been planted*

together in the likeness of his death, we shall be also in the likeness of his resurrection.

The Bible states that being baptized into Christ (not by water, but Faith in Him) totally defeats the sinful nature and washes us clean. It makes all Believers pure in the eyes of God. It cleanses all who have Faith in Jesus as His true Sons and Daughters in Christ. The price that had to be paid to defeat sin and death could not be attained through works of religion or by being a truly good person. It is much deeper that, seeing as how every man and woman is born into sin. This automatically puts all of mankind in the direct opposition of God. It took a perfect sacrifice from a truly sinless individual to unlock the shackles and free us from eternal separation from God. Jesus was that Person. He came into this world and died so that we all could be free. Our Faith places us in the Lord's death so that we could do away with the sinful desires of our hearts and be with Him. How do we know that we will be with Him? Just as we died with Him, God has also resurrected all Christian Believers as such.

Bearing Your Cross for Christ

If anyone comes to Me and does not hate his father and mother, wife and children, brothers and sisters, yes, and his own life also, he cannot be My disciple. And whoever does not bear his cross and come after Me cannot be My disciple. – Luke 14:26-27 (NKJV)

One of the most overlooked facts in our walk with Christ is the cross we must bear because we belong to Him. Christ never promised following Him would result in abundant blessings given unto us by men. In fact, he promised quite the opposite. In Mark 13:13 Jesus stated: "And everyone will hate you because you are my followers. But the one who endures to the end will be saved." The cross Christians must carry is mainly one of rejection.

Many still need to be shown the light of the cross and may reject the fact that they need to be reformed in order to be redeemed. Friends and family members may be hesitant on how to approach you given your newfound Faith in Jesus. Instead, share with them the joy of all He has done for you in your life. Do so by sharing the Gospel, which when heard can activate the Holy Spirit unto those loved ones who are currently lost. Find a common ground with them that allows you to open up and plead your case to change.

Another example of the Cross we are to bear can come from "a thorn put in our flesh," that the Lord will use for us to be at times totally dependent upon the Holy Spirit. The Apostle Paul testified to this revelation in 2 Corinthians 12:7-9, saying:

> *Even though I have received such wonderful revelations from God. So to keep me from becoming proud, I was given a thorn*

in my flesh, a messenger from Satan to torment me and keep me from becoming proud. Three different times I begged the Lord to take it away. Each time he said, "My grace is all you need. My power works best in weakness." So now I am glad to boast about my weaknesses, so that the power of Christ can work through me.

I love the fact that the Holy Spirit never tells the reader exactly just what this thorn was. He allows us to insert our own problems into the equation instead. This can be a disease, recurring sin, or any other sin that we seek the Lord for deliverance from. This is our cross, which we seek Christ for to redeem us and make us whole for the glorification of the power of the cross. If we endure unto the end, we will be saved, as stated in Mark 13:13. Pray to the Lord that He strengthens your shoulders for the weight, so that we can continue our fight of purification unto Him.

Remember the saying, "Must Jesus bear the cross alone, and all the world go free? No! Theirs a cross for everyone and theirs a cross for Me!

We Preach Christ Crucified

But we preach Christ crucified. – I Corinthians 1:23 (NKJV)

Many times, when I have seen and heard street preachers or other Christians witness to nonbelievers on the behalf of the Lord Jesus Christ, they mainly speak against sin and the sinful nature that all those outside of Christ live in. They spend more time trying to convict them based on guilt, instead of the Gospel of Jesus Christ that can deliver them out of it. This type of preaching is based on the idea that that Christians can scare a nonbeliever into repentance, without the actual use of the Gospel. The Holy Bible in John 17:17 states: "Sanctify them by the truth; your word is truth." That truth is that God as a man came to Earth as the Lord Jesus Christ as a sin offering for the sins of all mankind. This is so all may have eternal salvation through Christ, who paid the price for all who accept Him as Lord to be made sinless in the eyes of God.   When speaking of the Savior, we are to have a general knowledge of what the Prophets spoke of Him in Isaiah 53:5: "But he was wounded for our transgressions, he was bruised for our iniquities: the chastisement of our peace was upon him; and with his stripes we are healed." His genealogy of the bloodline of King David, from which He came from as stated in Matthew 1:1-17. His death in John 19 and resurrection in John 21 prove that His sacrifice was seen as good in the eyes of God and exaltation in Acts 1:1-10. This is the Gospel message that will cause a sinner to repent. Romans 10:17 states: "So then faith cometh by hearing, and hearing by the word of God." Jesus Christ is the word made flesh as stated in John 1:14:

"And the Word was made flesh, and dwelt among us, (and we beheld his glory, the glory as of the only begotten of the Father,) full of grace and truth. So preach Christ and Him Crucified before the masses so that they too will also begin to have Faith enough to receive all that God has given them in Jesus Christ...

Being a Watchmen for God

Again the word of the Lord came to me, saying, "Son of man, speak to the children of your people, and say to them: 'When I bring the sword upon a land, and the people of the land take a man from their territory and make him their watchman, when he sees the sword coming upon the land, if he blows the trumpet and warns the people, then whoever hears the sound of the trumpet and does not take warning, if the sword comes and takes him away, his blood shall be on his own head. He heard the sound of the trumpet, but did not take warning; his blood shall be upon himself. But he who takes warning will save his life. But if the watchman sees the sword coming and does not blow the trumpet, and the people are not warned, and the sword comes and takes any person from among them, he is taken away in his iniquity; but his blood I will require at the watchman's hand. – Ezekiel 33:1-6 (NKJV)

Ezekiel Chapter 33 describes the duties of the Watchman. The Lord appointed the prophet Ezekiel as a Watchman unto ancient Israel, to warn against the sinful iniquities of mankind coming against the Kingdom of God. The Prophet was to watch and warn the people by blowing the shofar (a ram's horn), which acted as a warning or announcement unto the Israelites. In this case, the shofar was used as a siren of danger about turning away from God unto their own sinful desires, and also unto false doctrine separating them from the Word of God. This passage of scripture is very important to the Church today, reminding believers to be ever so watchful against false doctrine creeping into the House of God. Many churches refuse to preach against sins such as homosexuality, premarital sex, and educating and raising our youth in the ways of the Lord. Many feel good messages are taught to keep people happy and comfortable in their current situation, giving them the false security that everything within is alright. This is often the case even when the Bible teaches otherwise. For example, Romans 7:18 states, "For I know that in me (that is, in my flesh,) dwelleth no good thing: for to will is present with me; but how to perform that which is good I find not." This warning is a upon all Christians, saying that if we are not watchful and vigilant, and willing to warn others against what we know is sin, we will be held accountable in the eyes of God. We must constantly – as long as we are in the flesh – remain conscience of the things we say, do, and give our time to in order to stay devoted unto the Lord Jesus Christ. This is not only for us but also our family members, friends and loved ones. Be watchful for the sword of the abomination and sound your shofar to give truth and knowledge unto the body of Christ.

Bearing Fruit for the Kingdom of God

There were present at that season some that told him of the Galilaeans, whose blood Pilate had mingled with their sacrifices. And Jesus answering said unto them, Suppose ye that these Galilaeans were sinners above all the Galilaeans, because they suffered such things? I tell you, Nay: but, except ye repent, ye shall all likewise perish. Or those eighteen, upon whom the tower in Siloam fell, and slew them, think ye that they were sinners above all men that dwelt in Jerusalem? I tell you, Nay: but, except ye repent, ye shall all likewise perish. He spake also this parable; A certain man had a fig tree planted in his vineyard; and he came and sought fruit thereon, and found none. Then said he unto the dresser of his vineyard, Behold, these three years I come seeking fruit on this fig tree, and find none: cut it down; why cumbereth it the ground? And he answering said unto him, Lord, let it alone this year also, till I shall dig about it, and dung it: And if it bear fruit, well: and if not, then after that thou shalt cut it down. – Luke 13:1-9

One of the main focal points of being a true Disciple of Christ is always remembering to set a positive example regarding what true salvation means in the Lord

Jesus. The parable of the fig tree is symbolic of the House of Israel, who rejected the Gospel of Yeshua/Jesus Christ as the Messiah, choosing religion over the Lamb of God. Jehovah God in return rejected the Hebrew people, scattering them across the nations for their failure to receive God's only means of salvation for mankind. This same parable can also represent the modern day Christian Believer, who holds no true knowledge of the Word of God. Being a true testimony of the Gospel of Jesus Christ will always bring forth righteous fruit that can in return be used to feed those who are hungry for the Lord. These *fruits* manifest in the Christian's natural life. They testify of the love and grace that God has for all who will accept His only way for salvation.

These *fruits* are clearly stated in 2 Peter 1:5-9:

And beside this, giving all diligence, add to your faith (belief in the Cross) virtue (moral excellence); and to virtue knowledge (of the scriptures); And to knowledge temperance (self-control); and to temperance patience (waiting on the Lord); and to patience Godliness (conscious of God's will); And to godliness brotherly kindness (treating all as you would want to be treated); and to brotherly kindness charity (Love). For if these things be in you, and abound, they make you that ye shall neither be barren nor unfruitful in the knowledge of our Lord Jesus Christ. But he that lacketh these things is blind, and cannot see afar off, and hath forgotten that he was purged from his old sins.

These characteristics will follow the Believer and show of the saving Grace of our Lord Jesus Christ. This is only made possible by placing our Faith solely in the Cross of Jesus Christ, who will in return grant us His Holy Spirit.

He will nourish the seed of Faith we have sown in Jesus Christ as read in Roman Chapter 8: "I pray all will take the time to water their 'tree' (spiritual man) with the Living Waters of God, Jesus Christ and bring forth much fruit for the Kingdom of God.

Speaking the Truth of the Gospel of Jesus Christ

Do not think that I came to bring peace on Earth. I did not come to bring peace but a sword. 35 For I have come to 'set a man against his father, a daughter against her mother, and a daughter-in-law against her mother-in-law'; 36 and 'a man's enemies will be those of his own household. – Matthew 10:34-36 (NKJV)

One of the harsh realities of being a true follower of Jesus Christ is the rejection of others due to your newfound Faith. When the Lord Jesus Christ came into this world, it wasn't to give everyone security to continue living their lives as they wanted. It was to let all know that there is a desperate need for a Savior. The Law and Religion are not sufficient enough to redeem man from the sinful nature bestowed upon us by the acts of Adam and Eve in the Garden of Eden. This revelation lets everyone know that all are sinners who fall short of the glory of God. Romans 3:23 reminds us that Faith in God will indeed cause many to reject you. No one likes the idea that they are wrong in their lifestyle choices and way of life.. Nevertheless, the standard of serving a Holy God is in fact living Holy. Service to a Holy God cannot be lived in any other way. This is stated in Hebrews 12:14: "Follow peace with all men, and holiness, without which no man shall see the Lord."

The Pharisees in the days of Jesus believed in following only the Law of Moses, and that this was enough to satisfy God. But they were only good in preaching and not at all capable of living by the Law themselves. Matt 23:27-28 reads:

> *Woe unto you, scribes and Pharisees, hypocrites! For ye are like unto whited sepulchres, which indeed appear beautiful outward, but are within full of dead men's bones, and of all uncleanness. Even so ye also outwardly appear righteous unto men, but within ye are full of hypocrisy and iniquity.*

The Gospel displays that one and only one is justified in the eyes of God and that is Jesus Christ, the perfect offering for the sins of the World. Hebrews 7:26-28 reads:

> *For such an high priest became us, who is holy, harmless, undefiled, separate from sinners, and made higher than the*

heavens; Who needeth not daily, as those high priests, to offer up sacrifice, first for his own sins, and then for the people's: for this he did once, when he offered up himself. For the law maketh men high priests which have infirmity; but the word of the oath, which was since the law, maketh the Son, who is consecrated for evermore.

Jesus came so that all of Humanity can be baptized into His perfect nature (Galatians 3:27) which places all in the right standing with God instead of a Law in which no man can keep, other than Christ Himself. I urge all to preach the good news that all will hear no matter the rejection. Upon hearing the truth many may not like it but will ultimately repent and be made right with God, as stated in 2 Peter 3:9: "The Lord is not slack concerning his promise, as some men count slackness; but is longsuffering to us-ward, not willing that any should perish, but that all should come to repentance."

Slaying Giants in the defense of the Gospel

Beloved, while I was very diligent to write to you concerning our common salvation, I found it necessary to write to you exhorting you to contend earnestly for the faith which was once for all delivered to the saints. – Jude 1:3 (NKJV)

As we draw closer to the end times – as prophesied in the Holy Bible – we persevere unto the second coming of our Lord Jesus Christ. As we move into this new decade, many false teachings, false prophets and unsaved men and women will come against Our God of the Bible. This will occur either by new New Age Spiritual beliefs or advancements in science that will try to sway our faith from the finished work of Jesus at the Cross. In Matthew 24, when the disciples asked when will be the sign of the Christ second coming, Jesus responded, "And Jesus answered and said unto them, Take heed that no man deceive you. For many shall come in my name, saying, I am Christ; and shall deceive many. And ye shall hear of wars and rumors of wars: see that ye be not troubled: for all these things must come to pass, but the end is not yet."

The end times will be of great sorrow, Jesus later went on to say. These times call for warriors in Christ to rise up against the spiritual wickedness that is coming, to be discerning of the events on the news, in magazines, and the music we are listening to. This is so we are not deceived into any false doctrine that will sway our Faith in the Cross. This is the time to preach the Gospel with authority to the world, proclaiming that Jesus Christ is Lord and salvation is needed for all of mankind by means of the Cross. I urge every Christian to study and stand totally on the Word of God, so that we are kept from the same judgment that will soon be coming upon this world. Believing on the Cross of Christ and placing total Faith in it will allow the Holy Spirit to guide us into all truth. John 16:13 states:

When the Spirit of truth comes, he will guide you into all the truth; for he will not speak on his own authority, but whatever he hears he will speak, and he will declare to you the things that are to come.

This will allow all who have Faith in the finished work of Christ the power to have authority over all devils, cure diseases, and heal the sick. This is stated in Luke 9:1-2. In addition, Ephesians 6:12, reads: "For we wrestle not against flesh and blood, but against principalities, against powers, against the rulers of the darkness of this world, against spiritual wickedness in high places." In the name of the Lord Jesus Christ, we will slay these giants and persevere to the end.

Jesus Christ the Same Yesterday and Today

Jesus Christ is the same yesterday, and today, and forever. – Hebrews 13:8 (NKJV)

Every Christian believer will find it very comforting that the Word of God states that the Lord is the same yesterday, today and forever. Simply by placing all Faith in the Cross, the doorway to all blessings secures our Spirit and comforts all who believe throughout the trials and tribulations of everyday life. No matter what manner of sickness, Christ remains a healer. Throughout much heartache, the Lord is still a comforter. And in much lack, Jesus still provides for our needs. The difficult part comes in believing to receive these precious gifts that God provides through our Faith that Christ died for all sin and has once again placed us in the goodwill of God.

Jesus stated in Mark 11:23-24 (NKJV): "For assuredly, I say to you, whoever says to this mountain, 'Be removed and be cast into the sea,' and does not doubt in his heart, but believes that those things he says will be done, he will have whatever he says. Therefore I say to you, whatever things you ask when you pray, believe that you receive them, and you will have them."

The lack of belief is what inhibits many Churches today who believe that the days of miracles have passed. This statement is both untrue and unbiblical. In the Old Testament, Israel had this same disbelief, which the Holy Spirit responded in Psalm 78:41 by saying: "Yea, they turned back and tempted God, and limited the Holy One of Israel." A lack of Faith in the finished work of Jesus Christ at the Cross, displeases God and very much limits the Holy

Spirit, who works entirely within the confines of the Cross. Romans 8:9 states: "But ye are not in the flesh, but in the Spirit, if so be that the Spirit of God dwell in you. Now if any man has not the Spirit of Christ, he is none of his."

The Holy Spirit works within our belief that Jesus Christ paid the debt of sin that we could not, and therefore provides us with His Holy Spirit. This delivers every believer from all manners of sickness or torment; if we only believe that Christ has freed all from the bondage of sin at the Cross. Disbelief often comes from waiting upon God to answer prayer in which we begin to not trust in Him. In the Lord's eyes, the idea is that our patience and prayer truly displays the proper Faith in the Cross. So in believing that Christ has truly freed you from the bondage of this world, stay prayerful! That even though the Lord may not answer your request right away, always display your Faith in diligent Prayer. Luke 11:9-10 reads:

And I say unto you, Ask, and it shall be given you; seek, and ye shall find; knock, and it shall be opened unto you. For every one that asketh receiveth; and he that seeketh findeth; and to him that knocketh it shall be opened.

God's Elect

And then shall he send his angels, and shall gather together his elect from the four winds, from the uttermost part of the earth to the uttermost part of heaven. – Mark 13:27

One of the most comforting facts about the Bible is knowing that we are God's elect, chosen by God to know the truth of His Word in Jesus Christ. This is what makes Christians unique from the rest of the world. Christians have ears to hear the truth and testify on the behalf of the Lord Jesus Christ. While the world rejected Him, we were enlightened by the Holy Spirit of God to receive the truth about Yeshua/Jesus Christ. We knew that was the sin offering for the imperfect man and woman. This is the *only* way to be made right in the eyes of Jehovah God (John 14:6)! This election was determined even before our birth. According to 2 Thessalonians 2:13,

> *But we are bound to give thanks always to God for you, brethren beloved of the Lord, because God hath from the beginning chosen you to salvation through sanctification of the Spirit and belief of the truth: Whereunto he called you by our gospel, to the obtaining of the glory of our Lord Jesus Christ. Therefore, brethren, stand fast, and hold the traditions which ye have been taught, whether by word, or our epistle. Now our Lord Jesus Christ himself, and God, even our Father, which hath loved us, and hath given us everlasting*

consolation and good hope through grace, Comfort your hearts, and stablish you in every good word and work.

The question now is what are we as believers to do with our election? Are we to just attend church on Sunday's and wait on the Lord's return? Or do we, as elected officials, have a job of service to our Lord? Surely, we must help spread the word of the Gospel of Jesus Christ to as many people as we can so the Holy Spirit of God can draw as many into the truth of Jesus Christ. We must let others know that Jesus Christ is the only way to God Almighty.

Chapter 2

Social Issues

The Holy Bible outlines the effects of the genetic sinful nature mankind has inherited from the sin of Adam and Eve. In the same case, the scriptures give many effects of this sin in our human bodies. The one who can help us overcome is Jesus Christ. Now let's take a look at the social climate that mankind has created in his fallen state. The sinful nature always puts us in direct opposition to the will of God. This opposition causes us to turn to other forms of reason to solve life's problems. The number one thing we must always do is believe in the Word of God.

Keeping Enduring Faith in the Gospel

And said, Naked came I out of my mother's womb, and naked shall I return thither: the LORD gave, and the LORD hath taken away; blessed be the name of the LORD. – JOB 1:21

In the events of the years since the attacks of September 11, it has become a dire need for every Christian to continue to stay faithful unto the Word of God, the Holy Bible. With the economy in constant decline, unemployment on the rise, and the evaporation of middle class America, our Christian Faith is always being tested by the Demonic influence that is in this world. As Job 1:21 states, Job had lost everything he loved dear in the span of one day. In verses 13-19 of the same chapter:

And there was a day when his sons and his daughters were eating and drinking wine in their eldest brother's house: And there came a messenger unto Job, and said, The oxen were plowing, and the asses feeding beside them: And the Sabeans fell upon them, and took them away; yea, they have slain the servants with the edge of the sword; and I only am escaped alone to tell thee. While he was yet speaking, there came also another, and said, The fire of God is fallen from heaven, and hath burned up the sheep, and the servants, and consumed them; and I only am escaped alone to tell thee. While he was yet speaking, there came also another, and said, The Chaldeans made out three bands, and fell upon the camels, and have carried them away, yea, and slain the servants with the edge of the sword; and I only am escaped alone to tell thee. While he was yet speaking, there came also another, and said, Thy sons and thy daughters were eating and drinking wine in their eldest brother's house: And, behold, there came a great wind from the wilderness, and smote the four corners of the house, and it fell upon the young men, and they are dead; and I only am escaped alone to tell thee.

Job's state of affairs mirror what many Americans are going through right now. This system of the world is slowly moving toward the birth of a New World Order, which no longer adheres to the Word of God. But the Lord is separating all who believe in the scriptures from those who do not. As believers, we must be more spiritually mindful of the omnipresent God who is at work in the unseen Spirit Realm. We must take heed to His perfect will for our lives, which was never based on this world's economy or social system. This is done by reading His Word, The Holy Bible daily, and seeking Jehovah in Spirit and Truth (the renewing of our minds and unto the truth, through reading and obeying the scriptures.) Faith in the Cross of Yeshua (Jesus) produces the real social and economic system that God truly wants for His children.

Philippians 4:19 states: "But my God shall supply all your need according to his riches in glory by Christ Jesus."

Vile Men

The wicked prowl on every side, When vileness is exalted among the sons of men. – Psalms 12:8,

The Holy Bible speaks at times on the environment of social climates. In the same way that Believers allow the Holy Spirit to move through them and shed light upon the world, the unsaved do the same. Those individuals who have a platform (such as athletes, musicians, politicians) are able to influence a society's way of thinking for the better or worse. Many people in popular culture inadvertently become enablers. An enabler is defined as someone who helps another achieve a desired or undesirable goal. For example, a popular celebrity can either be a positive role model by being virtuous and respectable, setting an example for others. Or a person of notoriety can be a liar, cheater or worse. Many weak-minded individuals will use a celebrity's status as a way to rationalize their own sinful desires and way of life. A great popular phrase is, "Whatever our leaders do in moderation, the people will do in excess."

In our world, a person of great fame and wealth, who is also a very sinful person, can become an enabler of bad intentions. A person's bad characteristic presents these same abilities to the general public as a way to be successful in life. An example might be a politician who is caught in a sex scandal, who can give someone a false belief that cheating on a spouse is okay, especially if they are otherwise successful. Or a reality TV star who is ungodly and filled with lust and foul language will give credence to our youth in how to act due to their celebrity.

A prime example of this is in the man Victor Crowley . Crowley was a New Age occultist and mystic who lived from 1875-1947. Aleister Crowley was very Anti-Christ and believed in doing away with Christianity. He wanted to issue in a new age of Satanic humanistic beliefs and authored a book called *The Book of the Law*. The book was written by Crowley while in a trance by a demonic spirit that he named *Aiwass*. The text was said to usher in an age of the free thinker's under the adage: "Do as thou wilt, shall be the law of the land." Aleister Crowley became popular among many musicians such as the Beatles and Michael Jackson. Crowley influenced them to indoctrinate others by way of their music, helping to usher in the Sexual Revolution, homosexuality and drug use in the '60s and '70s. I pray in this time, that we, as Believers in the Cross of Christ, set forth and be a prime example of the Lord in the world today.

The exploitation of Sexual Sin

For when they speak great swelling words of emptiness, they allure through the lusts of the flesh, through lewdness, the ones who have actually escaped from those who live in error. – 2 Peter 2:18 (NKJV)

As apart of American society, we are constantly being bombarded by images from TV commercials, pop-ups on websites, music, movies, and magazines. The introduction of these images into our subconscious mind is meant to awaken us to things we may or may not need in our lives. One of the main marketing tools many corporations use is sex in order to market a product or idea to the public at large. Why sex? It is the most used weapon by the enemy to lure believers and non-believers away from the truth of the Lord Jesus Christ. While sex between a man and a woman is definitely a beautiful thing within the covenant of marriage, when taken out of this context it can lead many to fall into the desires of sin. In this respect, sex is and enabler to the sinful nature that dwells within all of mankind. It just so happened when Satan designed the plan to destroy the morality of one's thinking, along with the innocence of the youth of America, He used sex to do so. He projected images into our subconscious minds through various forms of entertainment. Movies like *Sex in the City*, *40-Year-Old Virgin*, and *Wedding Crashers* all promote sex before marriage and dilute our way of thinking. They make many weak to the sinful nature that man inherited from the Adam during "The Fall." These movies play on the fact that sex is good and makes everyone happy, and that there is no consequence for acting outside the law of God.

While the pleasure is glorified the repercussions are not. They include the heartache of giving yourself to someone who only wants you for your body, the STDs, broken homes, and failed marriages that result from sex are never portrayed as the result of indulging in sexual pleasure. The same can be said for the youth of America, who dance and glorify musical artists who are sexually perverse in their own right in order to make money. This in return effects our youth by contributing to unplanned pregnancies, abortions, and depression. Children cannot handle having to make adult decisions at such a young age. Sexual enablers are all around us. That is why Colossians 2:8 states: "See to it that no one takes you captive through hollow and deceptive philosophy, which depends on human tradition and the basic principles of this world rather than on Christ."

We do this by keeping our minds focused on the Word of God (Bible). We watch just what we put in Our Spirit. The Holy Bible states in Roman 12:2 (NLT): "Don't copy the behavior and customs of this world, but let God transform you into a new person by changing the way you think. Then you will learn to know God's will for you which is good, pleasing and perfect."

The Influence of Spiritual Wickedness

For we wrestle not against flesh and blood, but against principalities, against powers, against the rulers of the darkness of this world, against spiritual wickedness in high places. – Ephesians 6:12

The term Illuminati or "illuminated ones," refers to a secret society that was founded by Adam Weishaupt on 1 May, 1776. The group mainly comprised of the rich and powerful individuals of German descent were advocates for free thought and secularism. They believed science, logic, and reason were the only basis of any true reason in the world. The Illuminati believed that man should have His own free choice without the influence of religion, authority, or tradition. In short, the Illuminated ones were early Humanists who believed that man is in charge of his own destiny and can in return become God by looking within oneself and finding Him.

In 1785, the secret society was infiltrated and disbanded by government agents on orders of Charles Theodore, Elector of Bavaria. He put an end to social groups who were secretly plotting to overthrow the Bavarian Monarch and Roman Catholicism. The Illuminati, like all secular and non-Christ belief systems, operate under the Spiritual guidance of Fallen Angels and Demon Spirits. Like Satan when He was in Heaven, they tried to remove God as the source of worship and ascend into the Heavenly Father's thrown. These Demon Spirits were originally the Nephilim of Genesis 6:4: "There were giants in the earth in those days; and also after that, when the sons of God came in unto the daughters of men, and they bare children to them, the same became mighty men which were of old, men of renown."

These Giants (Nephilim), much like Satan, seek to be worshipped by man as they once were before the flood of Genesis. God sent them to destroy the evil works of these Fallen Angels and to begin His creation anew with Noah, who was "perfect in His generations". This was due to the fact that neither He nor His family fornicated with these unholy Angels. After the flood receded, the Nephilim Spirits returned to the Earth as disembodied Spirits. They were half-human and half-angel, neither assigned to Heaven or Hell at that time. They began their corruption anew by using men and women who would open themselves up to be inhabited by them. This led to Nimrod and the Tower of Babel in Genesis 10:8-12. These Spirits roam about, possessing those in great authority in order to receive worship and bring about the one world government system, in which the Anti-Christ will rule over. This new world order will actually be the revived Roman Empire, which the Illuminati will bring about in the end time.

The Illuminati never truly disappeared after being infiltrated. Instead, they went underground to mastermind how to push their beliefs and agenda onto the masses of the world. These extremely rich and powerful men re-emerged as political figures, such as the Builderberg group, the Rockefellers, the World Banking System, and Trilateral Commision. Through their belief in Humanism, the Illuminati opened themselves up to be inhabited, either knowingly or unknowingly, by the Demon Spirits of the Nephilim, who were more than willing to dwell in the body of a rich, powerful individual and receive worship like in the days before the flood. The Illuminati use their influence over the world to promote Humanist ideas, homosexuality, abortion, and trends in modern culture that are in fact gateways to the demonic possession of unsuspecting persons. Their main objective is to pave the way for the

Anti-Christ to arrive on the world scene. But they must first turn the world away from Christ and onto the sinful nature of man for corruption of their souls.

So how can you spot the Illuminati efforts in our modern world, which will persuade many into accepting a false Christ? Please watch and listen to the YouTube video below, and have the Holy Spirit guide you into the discernment of the Satanic infiltration in our society.

Teen Pregnancy

Train up a child in the way he should go: and when he is old, he will not depart from it. Proverbs 22.6

I recently was disturbed to see on the news the enemy's attack on the youth of America in the form of teenage pregnancy. In a time when many parents are preoccupied with putting food on the table in our failing economy, this leaves little or no time for supervision of our young people. This offers too many evil spirits the go ahead to corrupt impressionable children, especially those who do not have faith in YHVH, Father God. Even in a time when we lack so much financially, we must never lose sight of our greatest resource, which is the future of our children. It's very important to teach and educate our youth on the Biblical principles that helped mold such a great nation as the United States. It also, important to remind children about sex education, which is ordained within the confines of marriage. This is spelled out in 1 Corinthians 7:2, which reads: "Nevertheless, to avoid fornication, let every man have his own wife, and let every woman have her own husband."

Sexual immorality becomes a detestable act which destroys the youth of a nation. It also harms the generation coming behind it, hurting the original plan of God by having one man and woman in a marriage covenant under the watchful eye of the Father. I pray that all parents – married and single – set aside the time to talk to our young teens about sex and the consequences that it can lead to. This includes not just unwanted pregnancy, but also death. It is time to stand and educate our youth, and save a child from a troubled youth and preservation of innocence.

The Sin of Pro Choice

I knew you before I formed you in your mother's womb. Before you were born I set you apart and appointed you as my prophet to the nations. – Jeremiah 1:5

With the way the world is going, the act of sin is not only more acceptable, but it is even promoted as the right way to live. There seems to be more actions and excuses for individuals who do not wish to take the responsibility of being a parent or taking accountability as an adult in the decisions they make. This includes decisions a person makes with their lives and bodies. One of the most important is that of abortion. I remember during the election of 2008, one of the great debates between each political party was about being pro-choice (allowing everyone the right to make the decision to have a abortion or not) or of being pro-life (the elimination of abortion rights). I wondered at the time who it was who gave us this right to choose who gets to live and who does not. This is the subject of taking of an innocent life who has not even had the chance to plead its case to the world. Many doctors argue that the actual life of a fetus does not begin until after the first few months of conception. But as Jeremiah 1:5 states, God may argue that case against the knowledge of man.

In the decision of being pro-choice, we are wrong! We are wrong to believe that we have the authority to decide for ourselves when and under which circumstances we can bring a child into this world. Several biblical scriptures back up this belief, such as Psalm 51:5, which states: "For I was born a sinner—yes, from the moment my mother conceived me." The Word of God says life begins at the moment of conception, and not months later as some would say. Regardless of what the natural world may tell us, we live our lives according to the Spirit, knowing that all things have purpose and meaning for our lives.

I did some research on this topic and found out that the most common reason behind the choice to abort an unwanted pregnancy is not rape. This only accounts for less than 1% of all abortions. Instead the most common reason is simple bad judgment. Many abortions occur because people feel they are not ready financially or mentally, or they just made a bad decision one night. So because we don't want to live with the consequences, we decide to take the life of an innocent child. I apologize for being blunt, but that is exactly what abortion is. The most responsible action to take is the choice to be aware of the consequences of our actions. If you plan to have pre-marital sex, use condoms or contraception before making a decision that will result in making another terrible one in a few months. Every life is precious unto the Lord. The creation of a life gives God great pride, because we operate as Him in doing so. When we were made in His image in the book of Genesis, God made us creators also just like Him. The act of abortion pollutes that gift in which God ordained us to walk in. It warps it into something very destructive. This was done also in the past in the book of Psalm 106:37-38, which reads:

> *They even sacrificed their sons and their daughters to the demons. They shed innocent blood, the blood of their sons and daughters. By sacrificing them to the idols of Canaan, they polluted the land with murder.*

This is speaking of when Israel worshiped the false god Ba'al, and to pay homage to Him destroyed the very children that they conceived for His "blessings." Another example comes from Deuteronomy 27:25, which reads: "Cursed is anyone who accepts payment to kill an innocent person.' And all the people will reply, Amen."

There are many more arguments to be made about why pro-choice is against the will of God. I ask that we all take a look into the world of God and see how wonderful life is if we submit unto His will. The next time this debate rages, just remember John 10:10, which states: "The thief cometh not, but for to steal, and to kill, and to destroy: I have come that they might have life, and that they might have it more abundantly."

Molech Worship

And thou shalt not let any of thy seed pass through the fire to Molech, neither shalt thou profane the name of thy God: I am the LORD. – Leviticus 18:21

Molech is an idol that was worshipped by the Semitic Hebrew people in a time of the ancient past. The idol of Molech was powered by an Evil Spirit, which received this false worship indirectly in the Spiritual Realm. This Evil Spirit demanded the ultimate sacrifice of its followers, which was the blood of children. It was said that this idol granted the establishment of kingdoms such as the Persian and Carthaginian, and protection unto the people from the heavens above. The worship of Molech was a very detestable act in the eyes of Jehovah God, due to the fact that it required the ultimate sacrifice: the blood of the innocent. Worship of Molech not only involved the sacrifice of children; it also opened the people up to a host of Demonic influence in the worship of the sun, moon and stars by Manasseh. Manasseh was the son of King Hezekiah, who built pagan altars in the Temple of the Lord for Satanic worship. 2 Chronicles 33:4-6 states:

> *Also he built altars in the house of the LORD, whereof the LORD had said, In Jerusalem shall my name be for ever. And he built altars for all the host of heaven in the two courts of the house of the LORD. And he caused his children to pass through the fire in the valley of the son of Hinnom: also he observed times, and used enchantments, and used witchcraft, and dealt with a familiar spirit, and with wizards: he wrought much evil in the sight of the LORD, to provoke him to anger.*

The idol of Molech is just that: an idol. It was constructed by man with no power of itself. But the Evil Spirit behind its worship is very real and demands the blood of our youth. This is true even today. This Evil Spirit manifests itself today in the form of child negligence and the desires of this world, which many parents and children want in order to provide comfort for their lives, instead of the Living God. These desires pull the young and old alike into abortion, adultery, and the love of money. These human wants and desires are not of God, but of the Devil himself. This Evil Spirit of Molech feeds off of these emotions and leads many into rebellion.

As Disciples of Christ and parents, we need to be aware of the ills of this world that cause us to neglect our children and discipline them to follow the right path which is Jesus Christ. We need only to share the Gospel of Jesus Christ with them daily and pray that His Holy Spirit moves within them to do what is right. Be warned and take heed from the scriptures about the neglect of our youth, as stated in Leviticus 20:1-5:

> *And the LORD spake unto Moses, saying, Again, thou shalt say to the children of Israel, Whosoever he be of the children of Israel, or of the strangers that sojourn in Israel, that giveth any of his seed unto Molech; he shall surely be put to death: the people of the land shall stone him with stones. And I will set my face against that man, and will cut him off from among his people; because he hath given of his seed unto Molech, to defile my sanctuary, and to profane my holy name. And if the people of the land do any ways hide their eyes from the man, when he giveth of his seed unto Molech, and kill him not: Then I will set my face against that man, and against his family, and will cut him off, and all that go*

a whoring after him, to commit whoredom with Molech, from among their people.

Effeminate Men

A woman shall not wear anything that pertains to a man, nor shall a man put on a woman's garment, for all who do so are an abomination to the Lord your God. – Deuteronomy 22:5 (NKJV)

The holy scriptures give strict rules and regulations about how children of the Most High should conduct themselves. One of the most overlooked is proper gender roles. In today's society, it is not uncommon to see men wearing earrings, carrying a bag that strongly resembles a purse, or wearing skinny jeans. This practice of the enemy is to emasculate men from the authority and image that God has given unto them. In return, if men assume more of an effeminate role, they lose their manhood in the process.

This is one of the examples in which Satan is destroying the family household. If men begin to look and act like women, this action in return forces women to step into a leadership role due to the man's neglect. In many cases, this causes a switch of gender roles that God never intended. The book of Genesis 5:2 (NKJV) states: "He created them male and female, and blessed them and called them Mankind in the day they were created."

The Bible states that we are created differently – males and females – and the line between the two should never be crossed due to any fad or fashion. Through the wearing of women's garments, the agenda of homosexuality is promoted as well, lending support to their cause and effort. If we are to inherit the Kingdom of God as Christian believers, we must properly reflect what God has ordained. The Apostle Paul addressed this in 1 Corinthians 6:9-11 (KJV):

Know ye not that the unrighteous shall not inherit the kingdom of God? Be not deceived: neither fornicators, nor idolaters, nor adulterers, nor effeminate, nor abusers of themselves with mankind, Nor thieves, nor covetous, nor drunkards, nor revilers, nor extortioners, shall inherit the kingdom of God. And such were some of you: but ye are washed, but ye are sanctified, but ye are justified in the name of the Lord Jesus, and by the Spirit of our God.

The original creation of man in God's original plan has never changed with the times. I believe it is time that we start allowing the Holy Spirit to direct us on how to carry ourselves in this world we live in; not only for our salvation but more importantly our Families.

Narcissism in today's Society

Know this also, that in the last days perilous times shall come. For men shall be lovers of their own selves, covetous, boasters, proud, blasphemers, disobedient to parents, unthankful, unholy, Without natural affection, trucebreakers, false accusers, incontinent, fierce, despisers of those that are good, Traitors, heady, highminded, lovers of pleasures more than lovers of God; Having a form of godliness, but denying the power thereof: from such turn away. For of this sort are they which creep into houses, and lead captive silly women laden with sins, led away with divers lusts, Ever learning, and never able to come to the knowledge of the truth. –
2 Timothy 3:1-7

Narcissism is defined as the inordinate fascination with oneself; excessive self-love; and vain. One of the main objectives of the enemy was to turn Mankind against its creator in rebellion against God and unto Himself to receive their glorification. This plan has been in fruition for the past millennium, with Satan and his Fallen Angels looking for the opportunity to lie and deceive many into offering their worship unto the Lord of deceit. Within the most recent years, his plan has taken taken off, namely in the crippling of the American economy. In times of prosperity, human beings are kinder and more trustworthy of people and their situations. But in times of strife and hardship, normal people turn selfish and more focused on helping themselves than helping their fellow man in a time of need. This same situation befell the children of Israel in the Book of Exodus, by them wanting to do more for themselves than for God. In this troublesome world, the people of today have done the same.

As stated previously, this agenda includes shifting man's focus from God unto himself, robbing himself of that perfect communion with God in prayer and meditation. Satan had this same frame of mind when he was Lucifer in Heaven. He worked to shift the worship of God unto himself. Isaiah 14:13 reads: "For thou hast said in thine heart, I will ascend into heaven, I will exalt my throne above the stars of God: I will sit also upon the mount of the congregation, in the sides of the north."

Narcissism leads to vanity and selfishness, two of the main qualities the Most High despises. This is due to the fact that the Lord wishes for all of Humanity to have fellowship and achieve oneness in worship. (Galatians 3:28 states: "There is neither Jew nor Greek, there is neither bond nor free, there is neither male nor female: for ye are all one in Christ Jesus.") In times of hardship, we should turn more to God instead of from him. For only He knows the right path for you to take and not yourself. I urge us all to take time away from your Facebook, Twitter, and Myspace to show love to someone else and let them know that God is still on the throne and Jesus still saves!

The Misconception of the Christian Celebrity

The devil led him up to a high place and showed him in an instant all the kingdoms of the world. And he said to him, "I will give you all their authority and splendor, for it has been given to me, and I can give it to anyone I want to. So if you worship me, it will all be yours." Jesus answered, "It is written: 'Worship the Lord your God and serve him only." – Luke 4:5-8

I have heard many times when a man or woman makes it big in movies or the music industry that it is a true blessing from God. It is said that the Lord looked upon an individual and gave him or her the fruits of this world. In some cases this is true, but in the majority it is a deceitful work of Satan. Many of the celebrities that we see on TV or in movies are actually pursuing the "god" of this world in an attempt to achieve money, fame and the recognition the world. What many people do not know is the high price one must pay in order to gain such recognition, which is in fact the worship of Satan himself. The sad truth is that the entire world is not Christian. Many people follow false gods and strange paths to enlightenment other than Christ in order to be redeemed. In effect, people must compromise the way that they feel in order to be accepted by such a diverse audience, including their belief that Jesus Christ is the only way to salvation (John 3:16.) The actual true religion of the most celebrities in Hollywood is that of Satanism. They either believe that directly or indirectly, by placing their Faith in Scientology, Kabbalah or eastern mysticism as their alternate belief system for redemption. This is the reason many celebrities begin by professing Jesus but soon after achieving success claim they have accepted false god worship over the true God of the Christian Bible. The reason for this is that only moderate notoriety is granted for those who profess Christ openly. You may get a role on a TV show, but in order to get the big budget summer blockbuster you have to sell out. This is due to the fact that God will not abide with the believer in the midst of such demonic worship. Exodus 34:12-14 states:

> *Take heed to thyself, lest thou make a covenant with the inhabitants of the land whither thou goest, lest it be for a snare in the midst of thee: But ye shall destroy their altars, break their images, and cut down their groves: For thou shalt worship no other god: for the LORD, whose name is Jealous, is a jealous God.*

In order to advance a career, a person may open themselves up to worship of a false god. This might their only path to that next level of celebrity. They may also involve themselves in drug addiction, such as marijuana, prescription medication and cocaine. These drugs open one's mind up to the influence of demonic spirits, which is why many music artists need to be intoxicated in order to be "creative" and land a hit record. Pray for all those who are lifted up as celebrities that the God of the Bible will keep them from such Satanic influence. As well as for the Youth who look up to them as role models, who may not be seeing talent but in return demonic possession.

Effectively Ministering to the World

Who hath delivered us from the power of darkness, and hath translated us into the kingdom of his dear Son: In whom we have redemption through his blood, even the forgiveness of sins. – Colossians 1:13-14

In this age of lost hope and faith, it is important for the world to hear the Gospel of Jesus Christ. It is essential that we as ambassadors to the Kingdom of God know how to properly relay this message to unbelievers. It's not about designing signs saying "You are a sinner! Repent!", though many ministers do so from street corners on busy streets. It's about letting people know they are forgiven. Jesus Christ's ministry, while He was with us on Earth, was not about condemning people for their sins. It was about letting them know that they have been forgiven for them. Let's take into account the woman caught in adultery from John 8:2-11:

And the scribes and Pharisees brought unto him a woman taken in adultery; and when they had set her in the midst, They say unto him, Master, this woman was taken in adultery, in the very act. Now Moses in the law commanded us, that such should be stoned: but what sayest thou? This they said, tempting him, that they might have to accuse him. But Jesus stooped down, and with his finger wrote on the ground, as though he heard them not. So when they continued asking him, he lifted up himself, and said unto them, He that is without sin among you, let him first cast a stone at her. And again he stooped down, and wrote on the ground. And they which heard it, being convicted by their own conscience, went out one by one, beginning at the eldest, even unto the last: and

Jesus was left alone, and the woman standing in the midst. When Jesus had lifted up himself, and saw none but the woman, he said unto her, Woman, where are those thine accusers? hath no man condemned thee? She said, No man, Lord. And Jesus said unto her, Neither do I condemn thee: go, and sin no more.

Christ did not chastise this woman because she had not yet heard the Gospel that He brought to all Humanity. We must view the world in the same way. Christians must first let nonbelievers know that Christ came to forgive them for their sin, and impart truth into their way of thinking. This is the way of the Gospel. It is not spewing hate at people, but ministering just what Christ has done in the Earth. Jesus said this Himself when speaking of His death and resurrection in John 12:32: "And I, if I be lifted up from the earth, will draw all men unto me." We must first let those who do not know Christ know that He has died for their sins, and the Holy Spirit of God will draw that person into repentance. Please make note that God causes people to repent not by our doings, but His! We can only tell them the Gospel and allow the Holy Spirit to spiritually awaken that person. John 6:44 says: "No man can come to me, except the Father which hath sent me draw him: and I will raise him up at the last day," and that they *first* must have ears to hear. Read, for example, in Revelations 3:20: "Behold, I stand at the door, and knock: if any man hear my voice, and open the door, I will come in to him, and will sup with him, and he with me"

God ultimately makes the decision to bring that person into the revelation of Christ now or later. Just know that you did your part as a Child of God. Not every person will repent at that time, but some will, receiving Christ with open arms. I ask that we stay with the scriptures when witnessing to the world that they have been forgiven, then once they have received Christ we can help them begin the purification process within.

Women Pastoring

In the last days, God says, I will pour out my Spirit on all people. Your sons and daughters will prophesy, your young men will see visions, your old men will dream dreams. Even on my servants, both men and women, I will pour out my Spirit in those days, and they will prophesy. – Acts 2:17-18

In my journey of searching for the right Church to worship with, I often came across some who believed women had no right to serve the Body of Christ from behind the pulpit. Many Churches still to this day promote the idea of women being servants unto their Husbands and remaining silent during service. This is stated by the Apostle Paul in His letter to the Corinthian Church. For example, 1 Corinthian 14:34-35 states:

> *Let your women keep silence in the churches: for it is not permitted unto them to speak; but they are commanded to be under obedience as also saith the law. And if they will learn anything, let them ask their husbands at home: for it is a shame for women to speak in the church.*

What many fail to realize about this scripture is that it addressed the social climate of that part of the world at that time. Back then, women were not encouraged to be educated or to be free of mind. Men and Women didn't even sit next to each other in Church services then, so when the Apostle was teaching, they would try to ask their husbands sitting away from them, for the meaning behind what was being taught, in turn interrupting the service by doing so. So to do away with this confusion, Paul asked the women to be quiet and wait and ask their husbands when they got home for the meaning of the message being preached.

Sadly, Satan has taken this scripture and used it for ungodly men to place our women into bondage and servitude unto them over the generations. Let us not forget that women were the first to preach the good news of the risen Christ in Luke 24: 6-9:

He is not here, but is risen: remember how he spake unto you when he was yet in Galilee, Saying, The Son of man must be delivered into the hands of sinful men, and be crucified, and the third day rise again. And they remembered his words, And returned from the sepulchre, and told all these things unto the eleven, and to all the rest.

Remember, there is only one stepping stool for all to use in this life and that is the Devil, and not our women! They are granted the same right to speak, teach, sing, and praise God for the Salvation that is in Jesus that all flesh should adhere to.

Judging Others

Let him know that he who turns a sinner from the error of his way will save a soul from death and cover a multitude of sins. – James 5:20 (NKJV) One very misguided teaching that Believers misconstrue is that of correcting brothers and sisters in Christ from doing wrong. I know that in the past when Christians try to warn or sway others from falling in their walk with the Lord, the term "don't judge men" always arises as a reference to Matthew 7:1 (NKJV):

"Judge not, that you be not judged." The scriptural teaching states that we are to correct those who are in Christ when it is needed, as read in 1 Timothy 5:20: "Those who are sinning rebuke in the presence of all, that the rest also may fear." If a saved individual allows himself to fall, or is misguided in their ways, we as Christians are to correct them. This also is to let others know that this road is the one not traveled in the scriptures. Matthew 7:1 actually speaks of condemning someone to Hell or guaranteeing Heaven unto someone. God (YAH) has that qualification and only Him alone to do so. This is stated in Romans 10:6 (NKJV), but the righteousness of faith speaks in this way: "Do not say in your heart, 'Who will ascend into heaven?'" (that is, to bring Christ down from above). Though we cannot speak of where someone's Spirit will end up eternally we can judge actions and beliefs. All men and women can repent at anytime from their transgressions and be made right by trusting in the Messiah to make them new.

In this case we use discernment according to John 7:24 (NKJV): "Do not judge according to appearance, but judge with righteous judgment."

Discernment examines a situation to see the righteousness of God in it. If there is none, we need to address this with the person first and warn others. The Holy Bible lays out clear lines for Believers to walk on in their journey in this life. When those lines become blurred, we should address them with scripture. In the end we are held accountable unto God for allowing our brethren to stray and not return back unto sound teaching. Ezekiel 33:8 (NKJV):

> *When I say to the wicked, 'O wicked man, you shall surely die!' and you do not speak to warn the wicked from his way, that wicked man shall die in his iniquity; but his blood I will require at your hand.*

God works in mysterious ways

God sent a spirit of ill will between Abimelech and the men of Shechem; and the men of Shechem dealt treacherously with Abimelech. – Judges 9:23 (NKJV)

Many may find it hard in today's society to see the hand of God working throughout the Earth, bringing about His will and sovereignty for His people. It may to some seem like there is no God, or that the Lord has turned His back on the people who truly love Him. However, the contrary becomes clear once we read and begin to understand the scriptures of the Holy Bible. First and foremost, let me say that God is omnipresent in all things going on in the Earth today. The problem that many believers have is that we are sometimes fed feel-good stories that God only does good things and if things are going wrong, we have failed to bring about His will on the

Earth. But the Lord is not always bringing love, peace and happiness to the Earth as we know it. The Lord still has a will and an agenda in which to fulfill His plan. This "Earth Age," in which we live is slowly but surely coming to an end, just as prophesied in the book of Revelations and countless other books of the Bible. God is at work in the good and the bad.

To those God loves, He blesses, but also to those He disciplines indirectly through different types of evil and good spirits. As in Judges 9: 23, Abimelech, who after ruling over Israel for some time, desired evil among the people. God sent evil His way, resulting in a revolt of the men of Shechem. The same is happening today in a world turning more and more unto their own ways and rebelling against The Most High. More and more evil is polluting our world. This evil will eventually result in the rise of the One-World Government and the Antichrist, which God has already predestined will happen in the end time. This evil is foretold in 2 Timothy 3:1-5 (NKJV):

> *But know this, that in the last days perilous times will come: For men will be lovers of themselves, lovers of money, boasters, proud, blasphemers, disobedient to parents, unthankful, unholy, unloving, unforgiving, slanderers, without self-control, brutal, despisers of good, traitors, headstrong, haughty, lovers of pleasure rather than lovers of God, having a form of godliness but denying its power. And from such people turn away!*

This is also evidenced in 2 Timothy 4:3, which states: "For the time will come when they will not endure sound doctrine, but according to their own desires, because they have itching ears, they will heap up for themselves teachers." God knows of this evil, and it is His will for it to come to pass in the Earth. Satan and His Fallen Angels are only tools being used to bring about what was already foretold. It is important to see the Lord in everything; not just the good but also the bad. It is important that we stay prayerful and warn those who do not believe (in love) that Jesus Christ is the only way and returning soon.

Chapter 3

False Teachings

In a sinful worldly society, many false teachings will arise to distort the truth. Let's not forget that the powers that rule this Earth want nothing more than to make the teachings of the Holy Scriptures of no power to the unsaved. The god of this world has entered into the Church to sow seeds of discord in false doctrines and rituals. Jude 1: 3-4 (NKJV) states:

> *Beloved, while I was very diligent to write to you concerning our common salvation, I found it necessary to write to you exhorting you to contend earnestly for the faith which was once for all delivered to the saints. For certain men have crept in unnoticed, which long ago were marked out for this*

condemnation, ungodly men, who turn the grace of our God into lewdness and deny the only Lord God and our Lord Jesus Christ.

The early Church leaders warned the people of God, that vile sinful men would distort the Church which soon many Christians would hold as Biblical truth. Let's take a look at some of these false teachings and see what the Bible says about each.

The False Teaching that Hell is not real

And death and hell were cast into the lake of fire. This is the second death. And whosoever was not found written in the book of life was cast into the lake of fire. – Revelations 20:14-15

It is very important to know in this day and age just what exactly the Word of God says on the very important matters as it relates to the second coming of the Lord Jesus Christ. I recently heard the Reverend Carlton Pearson speak on the subject of Hell during an interview, in which He stated that the doctrine of Hell is a "fairy tale". He added that it was a subject that is taught in many churches to persuade people to turn from their wicked ways and unto repentance to God. The Reverend went onto say that all souls – whether saved or unsaved – will return back unto the Father from where they came. This teaching comes from many pastors and ministers, who have a hard time believing that God, who is supposed to be a God of love, could not send anyone to a customized torture chamber for all of eternity. This defies the very teaching of the Holy Bible, which was written by the Lord's Holy Spirit through man. For example, 2 Peter 1:20-21 states: "Above all, you must understand that no prophecy of Scripture came about by the prophet's own interpretation. For prophecy never had its origin in the will of man, but men spoke from God as they were carried along by the Holy Spirit". And if God's Holy Spirit inspired the scripture, how can the Lord be made a liar?

Titus 1:2 reads: "In hope of eternal life, which God, that cannot lie, promised before the world began." Unfortunately, we live in and fallen World where many rebel against the very God who created them, due to the sinful nature with which all men operate. The Lord is a God of love but also of judgment. If God says there is only one way to Him, then He cannot lie and that one way is a true statement. John 3:16 says that we need Jesus Christ, and that without Him we are lost and must face an eternity of separation from God due to our unrepentant sin. The only "fairy tale" spoken of about Hell is that it is not a customized torture chamber where Satan and His Fallen Angels and Demons torment people. Instead it is in fact an eternal damnation for the unsaved, along with Satan and His minions. Jesus stated in Matthew 25:41: "Then shall he say also unto them on the left hand, Depart from me, ye cursed, into everlasting fire, prepared for the devil and his angels."

Hell is for the Devil. It was never meant for any man or woman to join Satan in eternal Hell, but those in fact have thrown in their lot with the Father of Lies to defy the will of God. It was never the intention of God to condemn man to this fate, but rather we chose it indirectly by not obeying His Word and not accepting the sacrifice of Jesus Christ for our sin. In some ways, Reverend Pearson is right. The "Lake of Fire" – or the final Hell – does not exist at this time. It will exist after the White Throne Judgment of God, which Satan and His followers will be cast into for all eternity for torment. I never like to preach about Hell. I prefer to preach the Gospel of Jesus Christ as a way of causing others to accept the Lord. But it is important for all to know the scripture and the truth about false doctrine.

Lilith

The wild beasts of the desert shall also meet with the wild beasts of the island, and the satyr shall cry to his fellow; the screech owl also shall rest there, and find for herself a place of rest. – Isaiah 34:14

Lilith is a Jewish myth derived from Gnostic (see blog below) teachings of the creation account in Genesis 1:26, Genesis 2:7. The Gnostics used these two accounts to implore their own dark agenda in creating the legend of Lilith. Their is no reference to Lilith in the Holy Bible with Isaiah 34:14 being the closes relation to the teaching. Lilith is taught as Adam's first wife. She represents the feminine dark side of Jehovah according to mystic legend. In having sexual relations with Adam, Lilith didn't see the purpose in always having Adam take the dominant position over her. This is the case since both were created in the same manner, from the dust of the Earth. Lilith rejected the position given to her by Jehovah and escaped the Garden of Eden to the Red Sea. When God sent His Angels to bring her back, she rebuked them and became a lover of Demons and Evil Spirits, eventually becoming a night monster herself. When Jehovah saw her demonic offspring, he waged war against them, killing most and enraging Lilith. She in turn went after Adam and his children, kidnapping and murdering them. Lilith seduced Adam at night according to legend, causing wet dreams, which she used to create more demonic creatures to torment the man in her way to get back at Jehovah.

This is clearly a myth developed in the ancient past that still lives today. Even though this is a false account, demonic spirits have inhabited this belief to receive false worship for themselves from God's creation. The myth of

Lilith breaks off into to several beliefs. Many women today see Lilith as the first feminist, taking control of her own future and not relying a man to provide for her, which is taught in much of the modern world. The second belief is that of keeping women servant unto man by many early teachers, and using this false teaching to control the women therein. These Evil Spirits control both ideologies to play the role of man and woman against each other in the world today. The feminist publication Lilith Magazine first published in 1975. Its website (lilith.org) promotes a Jewish-American publication that establishes women's rights that promote New Age agendas and abortion rights for women that go against biblical teachings. These Demonic Spirits promote Humanistic beliefs in women through this publication, returning them to the original Gnostic myth of Lilith. This Lilith teaching is actually used to divide the relationship between men and women, and destroy the institute of marriage, which Jehovah intended for all creation.

The Lord did not create two separate beings in the book of Genesis, but one. Adam existed as a dual being until Jehovah caused him to sleep. He divided Him into another separate creation, creating Eve in Genesis 2. Man is neither complete by himself, nor is woman. But the two come together to create the original creation, as God did in the beginning. I pray that no one allows Satan to divide the House of God, and for all to come back unto Jehovah through Christ Jesus (Galatians 3:28-29).

Humanism

The heart is deceitful above all things, and desperately wicked: who can know it? – Jeremiah 17:9 (NKV)

Humanism is the new Age ideological, political and religious belief that human man is God. This belief system essentially denies the existence of one true God. Humanism was established in 1836 in German schools. It was mostly based on philosophical beliefs that the Bible had become outdated. Humanists believe and teach that man needs to look within to find true self-worth, becoming the so-called "god" of his own life. Moral values are believed to be attained through experience. No one can teach a Humanist right or wrong; they must experience first-hand if they believe if something is good or bad. In short, it is up to the individual to decide about premarital sex, homosexuality, and any other sin. Humanists believe that man is constantly evolving, and that we descended out of the Earth and have now made it to this state of existence. This is also the belief of many Evolutionists. The statement of Humanism can be read in the Humanism Manifesto as: "We can discover no divine purpose or providence for the human species. We are responsible for what we are or will become. No deity will save us, we must save ourselves."

The beliefs of Humanism are inherently false, since they believe that nothing is spiritual and all natural. Christians know and believe that we exist in a physical state, but that we also have a soul and a spirit. A very crucial mistake made by Humanists regards the essential truth that one cannot look within to find good, because in the human nature dwells no good thing. Romans 7:18 states: "For I know that in me (that is, in my flesh,) dwelleth no good thing: for to will is present with me; but how to perform that which is good I find not."

We can only be made right through faith in Jesus Christ and Him crucified. Jesus is the only One who could look within Himself and find good. So in return we place our faith in Him, which will allow us to cling to His goodness by way of the Holy Spirit (Romans 8.) Spiritually, we join with Christ for the Father's will, as stated in 1 Corinthians 6:17: "But he that is joined unto the Lord is one spirit." Many men have chosen a path outside the will of God and have found death and destruction. Life was never intended to be based solely on personal experience. That is why the Holy Bible was written, to warn against trusting in a sinful nature of one's own belief. I pray that all Humanists return to the one true God through Christ Jesus who can in turn, "Create in me a clean heart, O God; and renew a right spirit within me" (Psalm 51:10).

The Atheist Agenda

The fool has said in his heart, "There is no God. "They are corrupt, They have done abominable works, There is none who does good. – Psalm 14:1 (NKJV)

Atheism is the idea that no God or deities exist in our world today. Atheists believe that man is the maker of his destiny and should not look to a higher power for guidance, which they believe leads nowhere except death and distorted truth. These individuals arise every few years, mainly around holidays that promote Jesus Christ, due to the fact no one really pays atheists much attention unless they are promoting something in a negative sense around the Christmas or Easter season. Satan uses these people to turn others against the Word of God and the Lord Jesus Christ. He gives them a platform in times when our country is in dire need for a Savior to rescue us from the pain of the world. They start discussions that promote the idea that Christianity is more of a plague than hope for the world. They argue about past events and miracles described in the scriptures as lies. Atheism is an ideology that leads to Humanism, which leads people to believe in oneself only and not God. Eventually, the world will be filled with the belief and set the stage for the Anti-Christ to cause war with Israel, seeing as how too many Israelis are causing most of the World's separation in the Middle East.

Atheism is a seducing Spirit as described in 1 Timothy 4:1-2:

> *Now the Spirit speaketh expressly, that in the latter times some shall depart from the faith, giving heed to seducing spirits, and doctrines of devils; speaking lies in hypocrisy; having their conscience seared with a hot iron.*

These signs are shown to let us know that the Man of Sin is soon to arrive upon a world, looking for a man to lead them into happiness and a better world, while being deceived into sin and death. I ask that we, as believers, minister to Atheist with love about just what God has done for use through Christ Jesus but never argue allow the Holy Spirit to move and if it be the Lord's will many will be saved.

Satanism

Whose minds the god of this age has blinded, who do not believe, lest the light of the gospel of the glory of Christ, who is the image of God, should shine on them. – 2 Corinthians 4:4 (NKJV)

Satanism is the ideology of a person dedicating himself to his carnal self and mind, into the self-indulgence of sinful acts. Satanism was popularized in America in

1968 by Anton Szandor LaVey, who wrote the Satanic Bible and started the Church of Satan amid the rampant sex and drug craze of the late 1960s. Lavey formed the foundation of Satanism based on atheism (the rejection of the belief in God or Spiritual Beings) to go against the religious institutions he felt many Americans were enslaving themselves to. He believed this enslavement robbed a person of life's more splendid pleasures. Satanists actually do not believe in Satan or God. In my opinion, their belief is a more radical version of atheism. The idea of Satan is viewed more as, "man living as his prideful, carnal nature dictates" according to Peter H. Gilmore, the Church of Satan current leader.

Satanists have nine basic belief statements. They include: 1) Satan represents indulgence instead of abstinence, 2) Satan represents vital existence instead of spiritual pipe dreams 3) Satan represents undefiled wisdom instead of hypocritical self-deceit, 4) Satan represents kindness to those who deserve it, instead of love wasted on ingrates, 5) Satan represents vengeance instead of turning the other cheek, 6) Satan represents responsibility to the responsible instead of concern for psychic vampires, 7) Satan represents man as just another animal, sometimes better, more often worse than those that walk on all-fours, who, because of his "divine spiritual and intellectual development," has become the most vicious animal of all, 8) Satan represents all of the so-called sins, as they all lead to physical, mental, or emotional gratification, and 9) Satan has been the best friend the Christian Church has ever had, as He has kept it in business all these years.

Also to mock the Church, Satanists invert religious symbols and ideas, such as the Cross of Christ (for example, in the picture above, instead of the Cross pointing up, it is shown pointing down mocking that Christ death and resurrection was in vain.) They also sing hymns that glorify the flesh and recite prayers backwards such as, "The

Lords Prayer," which in their mind reverses what The Lord has done for all of Mankind through the Cross. And sitting atop of the Cross is the pagan idol the Baphomet (a pagan god that resurfaced in the 19th century as a symbol of Satanism), which was derived from the scripture found in Leviticus 16:22, which states: "And the goat shall bear upon him all their iniquities unto a land not inhabited: and he shall let go the goat in the wilderness."

Satanists took this image as a representation of themselves, seeing as how the goat bears sin in which they choose to do also. In death they believe they shall receive the *gift* of every sin they choose to live in while alive. The idea of Satanism is very idiotic, as the first and only true source of Satan is found in the Word of God, and only there. Satan is not a rewarder, but an accuser whose fate is sealed. Satan is only awaiting the Judgment of the one true God. I urge all to please pray for any who are trapped in this deceit that they may be saved and receive Christ the true Gift of Life. Also please be aware of the rampant Satanic symbolism that is being forced upon the unsuspecting individual from music, movies and celebrities who practice Satanism either knowingly or unknowingly in their art.

Evolution Theory

And the LORD God formed man of the dust of the ground, and breathed into his nostrils the breath of life; and man became a living soul. – Genesis 2:7 (NKJV)

Evolution Theory is the scientific belief of the origin of Man and all life as we know it on Earth today. Evolutionary thought began around the 6th century with a Greek philosopher named Anaximander. But it really did not take flight as a genuine belief until the 19th century with Charles Darwin. Darwin rationalized that all life forms (i.e. human, animal, plant) originated from the same common source. That source was The Big Bang that some scientists believe created the universe in its entirety. Life began on Earth as prokaryotes organisms, which inhabited the planet 3-4 billion years ago. These eventually morphed into eukaryotes, endosymbiosis, mitochondria, plants, arthopods, insects, amphibians, mammals, and now humans. To many nonbelievers living in the flesh, this idea seems plausible. But to the elect of God, this belief robs Elohim of all His creative ability, which Satan has always been trying to do, according to John 10:10, "The thief cometh not, but for to steal, and to kill, and to destroy: I am come that they might have life, and that they might have it more abundantly."

In addition, many facets of evolution do not add up. Even much of the scientific community maintains uncertainty as to whether or not this theory is valid. While all life can be traced back to a single source, with many believing that complex life came from simple life forms, this is not the case with human life. According to the publication *Science*, (See MUFON UFO Journal, May 2001, pg. 11) the human genome has 223 genes that are not related to any other known life form on the planet; not even chimps as some speculate that we descended from. These very distinct genes are what separate us, and makes human beings distinct from animals, plants or insects. With no rational conclusion on how mankind acquired these specific genes, the only rational conclusion is that humans were created. When many try to understand and prove the existence of a Spiritual God, many can only come up with a big question mark! If anyone truly wants to understand the existence of our being, we only have to look to His perfect word, The Holy Bible.

Jesus did NOT Descend into Hell

And when Jesus had cried out with a loud voice, He said, "Father, 'into Your hands I commit My spirit.'" Having said this, He breathed His last. – Luke 23: 46 (NKJV)

A very misleading teaching that many Christian churches adhere to nowadays – namely those of the "Word of Faith" movement – is what happened to Jesus after His death. Many believe that the Messiah descended into Hell, where He was tortured by Satan until His resurrection. Many Pastors and Apostles teach that, in becoming sin, Jesus had to experience every bit of suffering that is due to man because of the sinful nature all are born into. They believe He suffered this through torture at the hands of Satan. While this seems like a somewhat relevant teaching, it is entirely untrue. Christ himself said in Luke 23:46: "Father into your hands, I commit my Spirit."

If the Lord said this, then His Soul/Spirit ending up in Hell would directly defy the scriptures and the integrity of Jesus Christ, making Him out to be a liar. Let's also not forget what the Messiah said to one of the two thieves who were also crucified with Him in Luke 23: 43: "And Jesus said to him, 'Assuredly, I say to you, today you will be with Me in Paradise.'" The more correct interpretation of where the Lord's Spirit was taken is Sheol, "the place of the dead", or Hades as it is referred to in the New Testament. This means the same thing as "the place of the dead." Sheol is a temporary holding place for those who have passed before the return of the Lord Jesus Christ, a waiting realm for The Great White Throne Judgment, which will take place at the end of this Earth age. Sheol or Hades is a place divided into two regions as read in Luke 16:26: "And besides all this, between us and you there is a great gulf fixed, so that those who want to pass from here to you cannot, nor can those from there pass to us."

The side with those who died in Christ is located in a section called "Paradise" or "Abraham's Bosom". The other is Hades, the suffering side of Sheol. Jesus went to "Paradise", the side where the souls of those who had passed from the Old Testament abided and preached the Good News of what He had done at the Cross. They took with Him those who received the message when He was resurrected days later. Sheol is not Hell. Hell is a future realm that is to come which does not exist as you read this blog now, as stated in Revelations 20:14-15. The suffering on the Cross and physical death were enough to take away the sins of the world with no further punishment needed. This was merely a sacrifice for the sinful nature of man. If Jesus went to Hell, God would not have recognized His sacrifice on the Cross as being good. This is due to the fact Hell is a place where the Souls of the lost are bound because of their refusal of the Gospel of Chris. He would have been separated from Him, which Christ never was! As

2 Corinthians 5:21 reads: "For He made Him who knew no sin to be sin for us, that we might become the righteousness of God in Him."

Some misunderstanding of Hell in scripture comes from which translation the reader is using. The King James Version of the Bible is good, but the New King James Version is a better translation to read from. This is because Christian scholars over the years have made more strides in understanding the Hebrew and Greek text, interpreting the scriptures clearer for a better understanding, and to rightly divide the Word of God.

The Spirit of Gnosticism

Beloved, do not believe every spirit, but test the spirits, whether they are of God; because many false prophets have gone out into the world. By this you know the Spirit of God: Every spirit that confesses that Jesus Christ has come in the flesh is of God, and every spirit that does not confess that Jesus Christ has come in the flesh is not of God. And this is the spirit of the Antichrist, which you have heard was coming, and is now already in the world. – 1 John 4:1-3 (NKJV)

Gnosticism is a spiritual movement that began around the 3rd century as a negative counter to the Holy Bible, in which the teachers of this religious movement inverted the story of the Old Testament. The Gnostics believe that all of Humanity exists in a fallen world created this way by an imperfect god who was banished from the Heavenly realms in a time past. The Gnostic story flips biblical teaching by making YHVH the one true God of the Bible and turning Him into the false god of this world. In other words, Gnostic teaching describes Him as the fallen angel Lucifer Satan. The Heavenly realms seek to free mankind from the curse of living in a tormented existence by sending Sophia a godly deity to Earth. Sophia uses the serpent to give us knowledge of who we truly are, creations of the false god who the Gnogstics call "The Ultimate Depth." Evil Spirits and Fallen Angels are the Spiritual force behind every false god or deity, hoping to receive worship as they once did in Genesis chapter 6, which is stated in Luke 11:24:"When the unclean spirit is gone out of a man, he walketh through dry places, seeking rest; and finding none, he saith, I will return unto my house whence I came out."

These beings are still constantly trying to receive worship by creating false teachings in which many believe. In return they turn themselves over spiritually to Evil Spirits. I do believe that we live in a fallen, unjust world, but it was not created this way by God the Father. Rather, it became this way due to sin, which was the result of man's rebellion against the Creator. The Gnogstics teach that Sophia wanted mankind to look within to find God in themselves to escape this fallen world. In return the world would be reborn in a more Spiritually mature state.

What Gnosticism failed to teach is that in us exists no good thing, that carnal flesh cannot be made righteous, and that true salvation comes from Jesus Christ, who entered this world to set all of mankind free, John 3:16. I ask for all to pray for those who believe this false teaching that they will come into the realization that Jesus Christ is Lord, the righteous of the One true sovereign God YHVH.

The Gospel of Inclusion

But even if we, or an angel from heaven, preach any other gospel to you than what we have preached to you, let him be accursed. As we have said before, so now I say again, if anyone preaches any other gospel to you than what you have received, let him be accursed. – Galatians 1:8-9 (NKJV)

The Gospel of Inclusion is a New Age belief, made popular by Bishop Carlton Pearson, a Minister in the United Church of Christ. Pearson began to teach a very distorted take on the finished work of Christ at Calvary around the turn of the century. This doctrine states that the death and resurrection of Jesus Christ granted salvation to all men and women whether they realize it or not. This "gospel" states that one does not have to believe in Christ to be saved, because Power of the Cross totally engulfs all Humanity without the need for them to believe or repent of sin. Followers of this dangerous teaching also do not believe in Hell being a literal place of torment, but rather a state of consciousness that we put ourselves in by not putting all our Faith in God.

On his website, Minister Pearson wrote, "A person who spends every day getting drunk will ruin their health, marriage, family, and career; they will make their lives a living Hell. But that still falls far short of the chronic alcoholic being condemned by a just God to literally burn in Hell forever and ever." This is very dangerous teaching because, if true, there is no need for Holy living. If we are all justified and do not have to repent of our sins, why not just live life the way we want to, indulging in every sin before we are called into perfect living by God. If there is no Hell, then the Bible cannot be the true Word of God. In Matthew 25:41, it clearly states: "Then shall he say also unto them on the left hand, Depart from me, ye cursed, into everlasting fire, prepared for the devil and his angels." Also Revelation 20:10 states: "And the devil that deceived them was cast into the lake of fire and brimstone, where the beast and the false prophet are, and shall be tormented day and night for ever and ever." It is true that the Cross of Christ did indeed justify all of Mankind, but only upon their recognition and need to be born again through the Cross

(John 3:7) and believe in the Lord Jesus Christ as the sacrificial Lamb of God for all sin Acts 16:30-31.

The Cross is all-inclusive but it is only through the small doorway of Jesus Christ. Matthew 7:13-14 reads: "Enter by the narrow gate; for wide is the gate and broad is the way that leads to destruction, and there are many who go in by it. Because narrow is the gate and difficult is the way which leads to life, and there are few who find it." I pray that all keep a spiritual ear toward sound biblical doctrine, and pray for those who have fallen by the wayside, such as Minister Pearson and His "gospel" that Love of Christ will once again convict His heart.

The Gospel of Prosperity

For the love of money is a root of all kinds of evil, for which some have strayed from the faith in their greediness, and pierced themselves through with many sorrows. – 1 Timothy 6:10 (NKJV)

I have seen and heard a lot of these popular messages from many so-called men and women of God, who claim that the more money you give, the more God will return to you ten-fold. On top of tithing, many spiritual pimps refer to offering up a sum of money unto God and He will bless what they have given unto Him and return back ten-fold. They almost always quote from the Old Testament about the Israelites, who were to give ten percent of what they earned as a form of taxation to provide for the needs of the Priests and Levites in the sacrificial system (these scriptures consist of Leviticus 27:30, Numbers 18:26, Deuteronomy 14:24, 2 Chronicles 31:5.) This is a false teaching that worldly pastors preach to rob many Christians of the money that God has truly blessed them with for their hard labor. This is what was spoken of in 2 Peter 3:3: "First of all, you must understand that in the last days scoffers will come, scoffing and following their own evil desires."

Since the Crucifixion of Christ, there is no longer a need for offerings in which to obtain the grace of God because our acceptance of Jesus grants us the pardon that we need. Nowhere in the New Testament does it nowhere state that the more money you sow, the more you will receive. In fact, in the New Testament, the Bible never states a 10 percent tithe to the Church. The Apostle Paul wrote in 1 Corinthians 16:1-2:

> *Now about the collection for God's people: Do what I told the Galatian churches to do. On the first day of every week, each one of you should set aside a sum of money in keeping with his income, saving it up, so that when I come no collections will have to be made.* – 1 Timothy 6:10 (NKJV)

This verse does not designate an actual amount, except that it should be "in keeping with his income." These are hard times for all, and the Holy Bible states in 2 Corinthians 9:7: "Each man should give what he has decided in his heart to give, not reluctantly or under compulsion, for God loves a cheerful giver." The best way to take control of your money and see a true return is through creating a budget and managing your money correctly. Pray and ask God to send a money-wise believer into your life to help you with your finances. Take these actions so that you do not fall victim to these dishonest "men of God", who take scripture out of context to fatten their pocketbooks at the expense of the Children of God. The Bible reads in 1 Timothy 6:5: "Perverse disputings of men of corrupt minds, and destitute of the truth, supposing that gain is godliness: from such withdraw thyself." If this message is being preached in your Church or Bible Study, have no part of it.

The only message that needs to be preached is that of Jesus Christ and Him crucified.

Chapter 4

Unfamiliar Bible Facts

In teaching the Gospel, we as Ministers tend to touch on the same subject matter. This is true even though the single most important aspect is Jesus Christ and the finished work at the cross. Many other subjects deserve some attention just as much. In my studies at different churches, I uncovered several topics that also need to be brought to light. It is very important that every Christian becomes a Disciple of the Word of God, paying attention to all topics and scriptures. In many cases, the topics normally not discussed on Sunday morning may be the very information a non-believer needs to become saved.

The Holy Spirit, the author of the Holy Bible

For prophecy never came by the will of man, but holy men of God spoke as they were moved by the Holy Spirit. – 2 Peter 1:21 (NKJV)

Many times when discussions about Religion arise, people who believe in a higher power but don't necessarily know who or what to believe, rely on the same question: "since all religions of the world are founded and recorded by men, how do we truly know who is wrong or right?" This is actually a really good question that every person should ask about just who or what to believe. It is true that all belief systems are written by man, but only one was written by men by way of the Holy Spirit of God. For example, 2 Peter 1:21 states that God used man to manifest His thoughts in the natural world by way of the Holy Spirit, who moved upon Him to do so. This allowed the true knowledge of God to be recorded without being biased to some sin, but rather that all have sinned Roman 3:23. A blind man would not condemn Himself because all men believe that they are righteous in their own mind. But the Bible condemns all Romans 3:10-11: "As it is written, Tthere is none righteous, no, not one: There is none that understandeth, there is none that seeketh after God."

Letting those know that we are desperately in need of a savior, which is the Lord Jesus Christ, who took our punishment for our sin to the cross and died. He then arose to show His approval for doing so by God Almighty. So the next time you hear a conversation about who is wrong or right, let them know the Holy Spirit of God is! The best-selling Author of all time.

Deborah and Jael, Powerful Women of the Bible

And Deborah, a prophetess, the wife of Lapidoth, she judged Israel at that time. And she dwelt under the palm tree of Deborah between Ramah and Bethel in mount Ephraim: and the children of Israel came up to her for judgment. – Judges 1: 4-5

One item many followers of Christ know today is how Jehovah God used some women in the Old Testament in the time before Jesus. We are all familiar with the New Testament stories, in particular Mary the Mother of Jesus and those who told the disciples of the empty tomb of the resurrected Christ. God used two women in the Old Testament in particular for a special purpose. They were named Deborah and Jael. Deborah was a Prophetess who was rose up at the time Israel was commanded by God to take the plentiful land of Esdraelon from a Canaanite army led by Sisera, a powerful Canaanite leader.

This story begins with Deborah calling the reluctant general in the Israeli army Barak and imparting in Him the Word of the Lord regarding what He had commanded of His people. Judges 1:6-9 reads:

"And she sent and called Barak the son of Abinoam out of Kedeshnaphtali, and said unto him, Hath not the LORD God of Israel commanded, saying, Go and draw toward mount Tabor, and take with thee ten thousand men of the children of Naphtali and of the children of Zebulun? And I will draw unto thee to the river Kishon Sisera, the captain of Jabin's army, with his chariots and his multitude; and I will deliver him into thine hand. And Barak said unto her, If thou wilt go

with me, then I will go: but if thou wilt not go with me, then I will not go. And she said, I will surely go with thee: notwithstanding the journey that thou takest shall not be for thine honour; for the LORD shall sell Sisera into the hand of a woman. And Deborah arose, and went with Barak to Kedesh.

Jehovah empowered a woman due to the reluctance of the Israeli Army commander Barak to carry out His commands. This speaks volumes that God uses everyone to do His will, not always men. The Lord looks for any and everyone who will hear His voice. He is not a respecter of persons (Romans 2:11). The battle commanded by Deborah played out in Judges 4:12-16, which reads: "

And they shewed Sisera that Barak the son of Abinoam was gone up to mount Tabor. And Sisera gathered together all his chariots, even nine hundred chariots of iron, and all the people that were with him, from Harosheth of the Gentiles unto the river of Kishon. And Deborah said unto Barak, Up; for this is the day in which the LORD hath delivered Sisera into thine hand: is not the LORD gone out before thee? So Barak went down from mount Tabor, and ten thousand men after him. And the LORD discomfited Sisera, and all his chariots, and all his host, with the edge of the sword before Barak; so that Sisera lighted down off his chariot, and fled away on his feet. But Barak pursued after the chariots, and after the host, unto Harosheth of the Gentiles: and all the host of Sisera fell upon the edge of the sword; and there was not a man left.

God was true to His word and swept the Canaanite Army from the land he asked Deborah to claim. The Lord utterly destroyed the all-powerful army that the men of Israel were hesitant to do battle with. In the end, only Deborah the Prophetess was strong enough and had the Faith to trust in the Lord for her strength. She was unwilling to adhere only to what she saw on the battle field. The destruction laid upon the Canaanite army was completely overwhelming, causing the General to flee the battlefield into a Kenite camp inhabited by Jael. Judges 4:17-24 records Sisera fate thusly:

> *Howbeit Sisera fled away on his feet to the tent of Jael the wife of Heber the Kenite: for there was peace between Jabin the king of Hazor and the house of Heber the Kenite. And Jael went out to meet Sisera, and said unto him, Turn in, my lord, turn in to me; fear not. And when he had turned in unto her into the tent, she covered him with a mantle. And he said unto her, Give me, I pray thee, a little*

water to drink; for I am thirsty. And she opened a bottle of milk, and gave him drink, and covered him. Again he said unto her, Stand in the door of the tent, and it shall be, when any man doth come and enquire of thee, and say, Is there any man here? That thou shalt say, No. Then Jael Heber's wife took a nail of the tent, and took an hammer in her hand, and went softly unto him, and smote the nail into his temples, and fastened it into the ground: for he was fast asleep and weary. So he died. And, behold, as Barak pursued Sisera, Jael came out to meet him, and said unto him, Come, and I will shew thee the man whom thou seekest. And when he came into her tent, behold, Sisera lay dead, and the nail was in his temples. So God subdued on that day Jabin the king of Canaan before the children of Israel.

The Kenite woman Jael was moved by the Holy Spirit to finish the mission of removing Sisera from the land taken by Deborah at the command of Jehovah God. Judges Chapters 4 and 5 show us that God uses anyone for the purpose of His glory, whether it be to command a Word such as Deborah or smite an enemy, as Jael did. God uses women as such today in the office of pastors, apostles, or those serving in the Armed Forces. God does not solely use men, as many churches falsely preach today. The Lord loves all His children who in return fulfill His divine purpose.

The Sons of Noah, Fathers of the Modern World

But with thee will I establish my covenant; and thou shalt come into the ark, thou, and thy sons, and thy wife, and thy sons' wives with thee. – Genesis 6:18

As a follower of Christ, I love to investigate the little known facts of the Holy Bible. One topic I rarely hear anyone speak of is how the world was repopulated after the flood of Genesis 7:10. At this time in human history, Noah and his family were the human beings who had not fornicated with the fallen angels of Genesis 6 to create the Nephilim Giants. This made Noah "perfect in his generations" in the eyes of God and the perfect human specimen to repopulate the Earth. After the waters receded and the ark settled onto Mount Ararat, the sons of Noah went out to begin humanity once again. The three sons of Noah were Japheth, Ham and Shem. The sons of Japheth

(Ashkenaz, Scythians, Riphath, Togarmah, Magog, Madai, Javan, Elishah, Tarshish, Kittim, Dodanim) are largely believed to have been the originators of the European and Asian people. This is based on Genesis 10:5, which reads: "By these were the isles of the Gentiles divided in their lands; every one after his tongue, after their families, in their nations." The "Isles of the Gentiles" are believed to be the British and Greek isles of today. The sons of Ham were Cush, Mizraim, Phut, and Canaan. The sons of Cush were Seba, Havilah, Sabtah, Raamah, and Sabtechah. The sons of Raamah were Sheba and Dedan. The descendents of Cush are believed to be the African nations of the world, which are referred to throughout the Bible as the inhabitants of East Africa. The third son Shem bore his own lineage (Elam, Asshur, Arpachshad, Arphaxad, Lud, and Aram). The children of Aram are Uz, Hul, Gether, and Mash. Arphaxad begat Salah and Salah begat Eber. This lineage is believed to have started the Arab, Aramaeans,

Assyrians, Babylonians, Chaldeans, Sabaeans, and Hebrew people. These are the beginning generations of the modern world, all different in many ways but unified in one humanity with different cultures. Most important though is the belief in the one true God.

YHVH the Sacred Hebrew name for God

And God said unto Moses, I AM THAT I AM: and he said, Thus shalt thou say unto the children of Israel, I AM hath sent me unto you.
– Exodus 3:14

Jehovah God commissioned Moses as His messenger unto the children of Israel so that they were to be set free from the slavery of Egypt. Moses replied:

And Moses said unto God, Behold, when I come unto the children of Israel, and shall say unto them, The God of your fathers hath sent me unto you; and they shall say to me, what is his name? What shall I say unto them?

The Lord responded "I AM THAT I AM," meaning I am what I will be, and I AM everything! This statement from God translates back into the Hebrew as the tetragrammaton (a word with four letters) as YHVH. YHVH – pronounced YAH Hoveh – was later deemed too sacred to be uttered by the imperfect man. It is a word describing all that God truly means unto His children who love Him. God is a deliverer, as read in the book of Genesis, He is all powerful (Genesis 17:1), God is knowledge (Job 38:39), Eternal (2 Peter 3:8) Holy (Isaiah 6:1-3) and a healer (Exodus 15:26). Anything that you need as a believer is totally within your grasp as long as your Faith is properly placed in the Lord Jesus Christ as your savior. Simply ask YHVH in the name of Jesus Christ for more of His divine nature and to open your eyes to His will for your life, and simply believe that HE IS, I AM.

There is no Sinless Perfection in the Flesh

I find then a law, that, when I would do good, evil is present with me. For I delight in the law of God after the inward man: But I see another law in my members, warring against the law of my mind, and bringing me into captivity to the law of sin which is in my members. O wretched man that I am! who shall deliver me from the body of this death? I thank God through Jesus Christ our Lord. So then with the mind I myself serve the law of God; but with the flesh the law of sin. –
Romans 7:21-25

Many Christian believers (and non-Christian) operate under the belief that a born again disciple of Christ should be perfect, Holy and sinless upon the acceptance of the Lord in Our life. This one of the biggest misconceptions about the Christian faith. It leads many people to be critical of the Cross and the finished work of Jesus Christ. The Apostle Paul, the Author of the book of Romans, still struggled after His conversion to Christianity, even after being Spirit filled and having seen the resurrected Christ on His way to Damascus (Romans 9.) In actuality, the sinful nature of man is only made dormant upon being baptized by the Spirit into Jesus Christ. The Bible reads in Romans 6:12-14:

> *Let not sin therefore reign in your mortal body, that ye should obey it in the lusts thereof. Neither yield ye your members as instruments of unrighteousness unto sin: but yield yourselves unto God, as those that are*

alive from the dead, and your members as instruments of righteousness unto God. For sin shall not have dominion over you: for ye are not under the law, but under grace.

In verse 14, the word dominion (which means rulership) says that sin will no longer control You as it did before, as every though that we had before the Blood of Christ was of iniquity (Romans 7:18.) The Word of God actually says none will be made perfect until the Second Coming of the Lord Jesus Christ, as recorded in Philippians 3:21. This is because the flesh is carnal and cannot inherit the Kingdom of God (1 Corinthians 15:50.) This is why the cross of Christ is so important. Even though we inhabit a sinful existence, the blood of Jesus places all who believe under the grace of God. When we do fall at times, we repent and turn from the sinfulness of our spirit. This why the Apostle says that after the cross in Romans 8: 1-4:

There is therefore now no condemnation to them which are in Christ Jesus, who walk not after the flesh, but after the Spirit. For the law of the Spirit of life in Christ Jesus hath made me free from the law of sin and death. For what the law could not do, in that it was weak through the flesh, God sending his own Son in the likeness of sinful flesh, and for sin, condemned sin in the flesh: That the righteousness of the law might be fulfilled in us, who walk not after the flesh, but after the Spirit.

Christ bestows perfection upon those who are imperfect based on Faith in His finished work on the cross. The grace of God, however, is not a license to sin by knowing that we are not condemned for it. Instead it is a reminder that even though we are saved, we are always in need of a savior. We should always look to the Word of

God so that we do not fall back and live in the sin that Jesus has freed us from. When we sometimes do not live up to the high standards of holiness, we should know that many believers still sin. As long as we learn from the trials of life our Faith in a perfect God grants us grace to overcome.

Nimrod Satan's First Anti-Christ

And Cush begat Nimrod: he began to be a mighty one in the earth. He was a mighty hunter before the LORD: wherefore it is said, Even as Nimrod the mighty hunter before the LORD. And the beginning of his kingdom was Babel, and Erech, and Accad and Calneh, in the land of Shinar – Genesis 10:8-11

The Word of God is adamant when it comes to preparing God's elect for the approaching end times tribulations. One such case is the story of Nimrod, the "mighty hunter", who was the mastermind behind the building of the Tower of Babel and the establishment of the Babylonian Empire. Nimrod was the first recorded individual to establish a universal kingdom. He made false doctrine to turn many people away from Jehovah God. In his pride, much like Satan when He was Lucifer in Heaven, he was lifted up due to his own greatness and accomplishments. As it reads in Ezekiel 28:15-16:

> *Thou wast perfect in thy ways from the day that thou wast created, till iniquity was found in thee. By the multitude of thy merchandise they have filled the midst of thee with violence, and thou hast sinned: therefore I will cast thee as profane out of the mountain of God: and I will des troy thee, O covering cherub, from the midst of the stones of fire.*

Though Nimrod was a very powerful ruler who tried to build a tower into Heaven, God ultimately intervened and caused distortion among His followers. He gave them different tongues in which they would speak in Genesis 11:5-8. Satan's plan at this time did not work, as is the case of other Antichrists throughout time (such as Nebuchadnezzar, Alexander, Napoleon, and many others). He finally will in one man and His number is 666, The Beast. The Beast will establish a great empire of every major super power government, to control the people and have them take His mark (way of thinking). As it says in Revelation 13:16-18:

> *And he causeth all, both small and great, rich and poor, free and bond, to receive a mark in their right hand, or in their foreheads: And that no man might buy or sell, save he that had the mark, or the name of the beast, or the number of his name. Here is wisdom. Let*

him that hath understanding count the number of the beast: for it is the number of a man; and his number is Six hundred threescore and six.

Rest assured that like in every other Antichrist, the Beast will not succeed; for the Lord Jesus Christ will intervene to do battle with the Antichrist and to save God's true elect from much death and hardships (Revelation 1:14-18). Take heed and preparation in studying the Word of God the Holy Bible, which in many cases proclaims the end times events with the greatest of all being the Second Coming of The Lord Jesus Christ (Revelations 1:13-18). Pay attention to the signs and keep your Faith securely in the cross of Christ.

Selecting the Books of the Holy Bible

The original canon (books that are divinely inspired the Holy Spirit) of the Old Testament were arranged by

Jewish Rabbis at the counsel of Gamnia. Their selection process was based upon the following criteria: 1) the content of each book had to harmonize with the Jewish Law (2) each had to have been written between 1450 B.C. and 450 B.C., since Prophetic inspiration was believed to have begun with Moses (1450 B.C.) and ended with Ezra, (450 B.C.), 3) the language of the text had to have been in Hebrew, and 4) the Book must have had been written in the geographical boundaries of Palestine. Any manuscript that met these criteria was included in the original 39 books of the Old Testament. Extra biblical books that were written around this time were the "Apocrypha (or "Pseudepigrapha"), which means false teachings. These books included The Didache, the Epistle of Barnabas, 1 and 2 Clement, the Shepherd of Hermas, the Apocalypse of Peter, and the Acts of Paul. These did bear some truth, but were not believed to have been divinely inspired by God.

At the beginning of the 3rd century, 22 new books (which would comprise our New Testament) became widely accepted. The criteria for the New Testament books were 1) it had to have been written by an Apostle, (2) the content of the book had to be spiritual 3) the book had to have been received by the Church and 4) the text had to bear witness to Divine inspiration. This later led to the inclusion of five more books (Hebrews, James, 2 Peter, 2 John, and 3 John), which became the authorative Holy Bible. Even though the selection process was done by man, let's not forget that all scripture is inspired by the Holy Spirit (2 Peter 1:21), who inspired man to record the Word of God.

Dinosaurs in the Bible

Take a look at Behemoth,which I made, just as I made you. It eats grass like an ox. See its powerful loins and the muscles of its belly. Its tail is as strong as a cedar. The sinews of its thighs are knit tightly together. Its bones are tubes of bronze. Its limbs are bars of iron. It is a prime example of God's handiwork, and only its Creator can threaten it. The mountains offer it their best food, where all the wild animals play. It lies under the lotus plants, hidden by the reeds in the marsh. The lotus plants give it shade among the willows beside the stream. It is not disturbed by the raging river, not concerned when the swelling Jordan rushes around it. No one can catch it off guard or put a ring in its nose and lead it away. – Job 40:15-24

Over the years I often heard many people question the Bible on certain subjects and dinosaurs are one of them. Since modern science states that these ancient reptiles roamed the Earth long before man, I searched the book of

Genesis, which I believed to be the oldest book of the Bible. At that point an old Christian friend of mine pointed me to the book of Job in the Holy Bible. Upon reading, I was amazed to find out that the book of Job not only gives a very good description of a dinosaur-like creature listed in the above scripture simply known as "Behemoth", I learned that the book of Job actually predates the book of Genesis by 650 years! This old text was written by an unknown Israelite around 2150 BC and gives very interesting facts regarding the interaction between Job, God, and Satan. This account takes place before the Earth became null and void as stated in Genesis 1:2, in which some otherworldly disaster destroyed the Earth. Take the time to share this with non-believers and continue to search your Bibles for the truth of God. Always remember Hosea 4:6, which states: "My people are destroyed for lack of knowledge."

Chapter 5

End Times Prophecy

The Holy Bible is one of the few sources on Earth to document the origin of the Human Earth Age along with the ending. Whereas the unsaved world is unsure of just what lies ahead, we can be comforted in the return of Jesus Christ the Messiah. The book of Revelations along with Ezekiel gives an in depth account of just how things will end and how Jesus will bring the total redemption of mankind. In the study of the book of Revelations and of the Prophets, it is very important to discern the times we live in to become fruitful Watchmen of the Lord.

The Rapture of the Church

After that, we who are still alive and are left will be caught up together with them in the clouds to meet the Lord in the air. And so we will be with the Lord forever. – 1 Thessalonians 4: 17

The Rapture, which is spoken of in the New Testament of the Holy Bible, refers to the churches who truly serve Jesus Christ and who will be caught up in the sky to meet the Lord during the tribulation period. The term *rapture* is not actually stated in scripture when describing this event. Rather, it is used instead of the term "caught up" as in The Holy Bible. At this time, those who have passed and were in Christ, and those who are still living, will be given glorified bodies and meet The Christ in the sky. This is stated in 1 Corinthians 15: 52-52, which reads: "Behold, I show you a mystery; We shall not all sleep, but we shall

all be changed, In a moment, in the twinkling of an eye, at the last trump: for the trumpet shall sound, and the dead shall be raised incorruptible, and we shall be changed."

The Lord Jesus purpose during this event is to provide an escape from the coming judgment of God upon the rest of the world; especially those who have received the mark of the beast (please read below for more on the mark of the beast) under His New World government. Many Christians should be aware that the rapture will not occur before the coming of the Antichrist but after, once He is empowered by Satan Himself. So please be ready. The Bible speaks of these troublesome times in 2 Timothy 3: 1-7, in which our faith will be tempted. But as the Word of God states in Luke 21:28: "And when these things begin to come to pass, then look up, and lift up your heads; for your redemption draweth nigh."

The tribulation period will be a period of 7 years, as stated in Daniel 9:24-27, 3 and one half years of peace then 3 and one half of torment. I believe that it is after the first half when those who are in Christ will be "caught up" to receive our glorified bodies and go with Jesus, returning after to do away with Satan and His Fallen Angels and the sinful New World government. During this first period of three and a half years, it is expedient that we preach the gospel of Jesus Christ and Him Crucified so that those who have ears to hear will be raptured up with us to meet the Lord in the sky. So do not fear anything when these events begin to unfold in front of our eyes in newspapers and on television. As 1 Thessalonians 4:18 reads: "Therefore encourage each other with these words. "Meaning that Our Lord Jesus Christ is very soon to come, and free all who are in Him dead and alive from the Devil and the bondage of sin.

The Second Coming of the Glorified Christ

His head and his hairs were white like wool, as white as snow; and his eyes were as a flame of fire; And his feet like unto fine brass, as if they burned in a furnace; and his voice as the sound of many waters. And he had in his right hand seven stars: and out of his mouth went a sharp twoedged sword: and his countenance was as the sun shineth in his strength. And when I saw him, I fell at his feet as dead. And he laid his right hand upon me, saying unto me, Fear not; I am the first and the last: I am he that liveth, and was dead; and, behold, I am alive for evermore, Amen; and have the keys of hell and of death. – Revelation 1:14-18

There is no description in the Holy Bible (Old Testament or New) that describes just what exactly the

Lord Jesus Christ looked like, when He walked the Earth as man during His Earthly ministry. The Book of Revelations does, however, give us a glimpse of how the Christ will look in His second coming. Revelation 1:14-18 describes His head and hair as "white like wool" (Representing His Majesty and Authority) and having the eyes of "flame of fire" (which represents penetrating scrutiny and fierce judgment.) The Second Coming of Jesus Christ will be one of Judgment. It will be a blessing for all who have believed in the finished work that He accomplished at the cross in the years past. This coming, unlike the First as the Lamb, will be as a lion to finally do away with Satan and His Fallen Angels, and those who follow Him in acts of sin. "And His feet like unto fine brass" signifies the Humanity of Jesus although glorified now, and having the voice of "many waters signifies the the voice of power. The Lord will return with all Glory and power that He arose with

2,000 years ago to pass Judgment and usher in the New Kingdom Age.

John the Revelator fell at the feet of Jesus "as if dead" due to the authority at which the very presence will have comforting those who have waited so long to be in His presence. This will signify to those who never believed that Jesus Christ is Lord! We find that comfort in verse 18, which states "I am he that liveth, and was dead; and, behold, I am alive for evermore, Amen; and have the keys of hell and of death." Christ is stating here that He lives, and will never die again, and brings with Him life. Though He was dead, He entered into death (our death) and finished the sacrifice for all sin. He was arisen by God and death now is totally defeated! Through faith in the work of the cross, we entered into this death Spiritually and can now also be alive just as Jesus now is. (Romans 6:3-5) Jesus now has the keys to Hell and Death, and the right now to pass Judgment on all who carry sin and the separation from God. I pray that all will do their part to spread the good news of the cross of Christ to all who have ears to hear the Gospel of Christ and Eternal Life.

Anti-Christ, the False Messiah

And I stood upon the sand of the sea, and saw a beast rise up out of the sea, having seven heads and ten horns, and upon his horns ten crowns, and upon his heads the name of blasphemy. And the beast which I saw was like unto a leopard, and his feet were as the feet of a bear, and his mouth as the mouth of a lion: and the dragon gave him his power, and his seat, and great authority. – Revelations 13:1-2

The book of Revelations reveals Satan's last great deception to deceive mankind into the practice of false god worship. This He does in exalting himself as the one true God. The Antichrist is the Devil's main person of interest in his unholy trinity (with Satan as God, the Antichrist as

Jesus, and the False Prophet as the Holy Spirit.) The Antichrist, unlike many teachings about him, will not be a religious figure but more of a charismatic political leader. He will have great influence in the world we know today. Upon arriving on the world stage, the devil incarnate will first appear as a peacekeeper. However, He will morph into something entirely different from what he first appeared. Revelations 13 speaks of the Antichrist appearing "upon the sand of the sea" (the sea represents the people) and having seven heads and ten horns (this represents the seven empires that have persecuted Israel in the past, with the "ten horns" actually meaning the seventh head; the "ten horns" representing ten nations yet to come.)

The crowns spoken of here as "being crowned" means that these nations have come to power and will use their political means to aid the Antichrist. These nations will be located in the Middle East, parts of Europe, and North Africa, all being part of the old Roman Empire territory (Daniel 7:7-8.) The book of Daniel gives us insight upon His arrival as a world power in Daniel 11:36-37 by stating:

> *And the king shall do according to his will; and he shall exalt himself, and magnify himself above every god, and shall speak marvellous things against the God of gods, and shall prosper till the indignation be accomplished: for that that is determined shall be done. Neither shall he regard the God of his fathers, nor the desire of women, nor regard any god: for he shall magnify himself above all.*

This is much like Lucifer, who became prideful upon his position in Heaven and made the attempt to direct the worship toward himself and instead of God (Ezekiel 28). The Antichrist will be an extreme humanist (glorification of self), who will glorify himself over all, regardless of religion or even the need for women. This is why I believe the homosexual agenda is being pushed so hard in the world today, with it being a sign of the coming false Christ. The Antichrist will turn his wrath toward Israel and the nations of the world, demanding servitude and obedience unto his ungodly will. Luckily for the church, we will not see the Antichrist come into power. According to 2 Thessalonians 2:7-9:

> *For the secret power of lawlessness is already at work; but the one who now holds it back will continue to do so till he is taken out of the way. And then the lawless one will be revealed, whom the Lord Jesus will overthrow with the breath of his mouth and destroy by the splendor of his coming.*

The coming of the lawless one will be in accordance with the work of Satan, as displayed in all kinds of counterfeit miracles, signs and wonders. The "One who holds back", or the power lawless one (Antichrist), is the church, which will be "taken away" or raptured up. The Antichrist will be empowered by Satan, having lying signs and wonders. But the forces of darkness will not prevail, as stated in 2 Thessalonins 8, which says: "WHOM THE LORD WILL CONSUME WITH THE SPIRIT OF HIS MOUTH, AND SHALL DESTROY WITH THE BRIGHTNESS OF HIS COMING.:

It is important to know that all false doctrine, false worship (e.g. celebrities) and humanist self-promotion is all one and the same. This promotes the Antichrist spirit coming into the world. Every Christian needs to spread the truth of the Gospel, which is of Jesus Christ and Him crucified, so that the world may escape the tribulations of the Antichrist and experience the joy of the Lord Jesus

The Mysterious Mark of the Beast Revealed

So what is the mark of the Beast? Whatever it is will be required of all who wish to prosper under the New World Government, which is soon to come. This actually is represented by the return of the old Roman Empire. Whoever accepts it will bring the very wrath of God down upon them during the second coming of Christ, per Revelation 14:9-10. I know that the preconceived notion is that the mark of the Beast, which is 666 (Revelations 13:16-18) will be embedded on the forehead or on the hand by those who accept it, whether by tattoo or a bar code planted on the skin. This is partially false information, though something to this effect may happen. The Bible states that the mark has been around for centuries (Revelations 20:4). Revelation 14:10 states: "must drink the wine of God's anger. It has been poured full strength into God's cup of wrath. And they will be tormented with fire and burning sulfur in the presence of the holy angels and the Lamb."

We really have to look at just what the Bible says about those who are the recipients God's anger. Colossians 3:6 reads: "For which things' sake the wrath of God cometh on the children of disobedience." The Mark of the Beast is plainly stated as a brand of disobedience of everything that is of God! By comparison, God ordained a contrasting mark of obedience upon ancient Israel in Exodus 31:13-17:

> *Speak thou also unto the children of Israel, saying, Verily my sabbaths ye shall keep: for it is a sign between me and you throughout your generations; that ye may know that I am the LORD that doth sanctify you. Ye shall keep the sabbath therefore; for it is holy unto you: every one that defileth it shall surely be put to death: for whosoever*

doeth any work therein, that soul shall be cut off from among his people. Six days may work be done; but in the seventh is the sabbath of rest, holy to the LORD: whosoever doeth any work in the sabbath day, he shall surely be put to death. Wherefore the children of Israel shall keep the sabbath, to observe the sabbath throughout their generations, for a perpetual covenant. It is a sign between me and the children of Israel for ever: for in six days the LORD made heaven and earth, and on the seventh day he rested, and was refreshed.

Their minds and actions were set to truly observe Him on this day. Revelations 13:16-18 explains the Mark of the Beast further:

He required everyone—small and great, rich and poor, free and slave—to be given a mark on the right hand or on the forehead. And no one could buy or sell anything without that mark, which was either the name of the beast or the number representing his name. Wisdom is needed here. Let the one with understanding solve the meaning of the number of the beast, for it is the number of a man. His number is 666.

Deuteronomy 6:8 states another mark of obedience unto God, that of His commandments. These were given to Moses, who stated: "And thou shalt bind them for a sign upon thine hand, and they shall be as frontlets between thine eyes." The hand is symbolic of your actions (works) while the forehead represents your intellect. This meaning that the mark of the Beast is taken by anyone who believes in any law contrary to the word of God (mark on the forehead) and takes actions upon it (right hand). Your beliefs and actions will cause you to take the mark of the

Beast, though not a specific brand or mark. In conclusion, the Bible gives references to two marks and describes how one receives it. One is of God, and the other is that of Satan. In the last days, all Christian brother and sisters need to stand fast on the total word of God and attain knowledge of every scripture, so that he or she will have all understanding of the events that are soon to come! This is so that we will not believe falsehoods or take actions against the very Law of God. I pray that the Lord will keep His mark upon all of us.

The False Prophet

And I beheld another beast coming up out of the Earth; and he had two horns like a lamb, and he spake as a dragon. And he exerciseth all the power of the first beast before him, and causeth the earth and them which dwell therein to worship the first beast, whose deadly wound was healed. And he doeth great wonders, so that he maketh fire come down from heaven on the earth in the sight of men, And deceiveth them that dwell on the earth by the means of those miracles which he had power to do in the sight of the beast; saying to them that dwell on the earth, that they should make an image to the beast, which had the wound by a sword, and did live. And he had power to give life unto the image of the beast, that the image of the beast should both speak, and cause that as many as would not worship the image of the beast should be killed. – Revelation 13:11-15

The Book of Revelations refers to the false prophet as the second Beast of Satan's unholy trinity (represented with Satan as God, the Antichrist as Jesus and the False Prophet as the Holy Spirit). This is revealed by John the Revelator. In the Devil's last effort to deceive humanity,

He will counterfeit a false Christ just as God sent the true Messiah in a time past in Jesus Christ. And just as how John the Baptist paved the way for Jesus, the False Prophet will do the same for the Antichrist. The word *Earth*, as described in verse 11, is symbolic of the false prophet not being sent from God but from the world. The lamb-like appearance of the prophet is intended to deceive many into believing that He is innocent. However, he will be powered by Satan Himself.

Satan's prophet will turn out to be blasphemous, as anointed by Him speaking as a dragon and greatly promoting the demonic Antichrist as the Savior of the world. This same practice can be seen and heard in many churches today that have placed their faith in things other than the cross of Christ as their means of salvation. The Holy Bible states that this prophet will not only having a persuasive tongue, but also have demonic powers. This is read in Revelations 13:13, which states: "And he doeth great wonders, so that he maketh fire come down from heaven on the earth in the sight of men." This will be achieved through Satan and his fallen angels. The "deadly wound" mentioned in verse 12 will not be of a assassination attempt on the Antichrist. Rather this represents a powerful fallen angel who helped bring the Greek Empire into power under the rule of Alexander the Great and has been since locked away. In this verse it is released to aid the false Christ in his world domination. This wound being "healed" speaks of this fallen angel's release (Dan 7:6, Rev. 11:7, 13:2). Revelation 13:14 does allude to the Antichrist being wounded, "which had the wound by a sword, and did live". This will be some type of mortal wound, in which the Antichrist will survive, giving Him the aura of being invincible and divinely anointed. The Word of God does not exactly reveal who this false prophet is, but does allude to the fact that He will be some type of religious figure. It could be pastor or minister, but I believe more or less that He will be a future pope. This is due to the fact that a pope has both religious and political ties to the world, which would have great influence in persuading the world in accepting the false Christ. This may be why Pope Benedict XVI is urging Christians, Muslims and Jews to reconcile their differences to promote peace in the world. Whoever this individual turns out to be, always know that any true minister, pastor, or apostle will only give credit to the true Gospel of Jesus Christ, which is Him crucified (1 Corinthians 1:23). Be attentive as we approach the last days that no man deceive you. So that the one true God can keep you, only by your Faith being placed in Jesus Christ and Him crucified.

The Two Witnesses

And I will give power unto my two witnesses, and they shall prophesy a thousand two hundred and threescore days, clothed in sackcloth. These are the two olive trees, and the two candlesticks standing before the God of the Earth. – Revelation 11:3-4

John, the author of the Revelation of Jesus Christ, describes two Holy witnesses of the Lord Jesus Christ, who will arise during the last half of the Great Tribulation and give powerful testimony on the behalf of the Lord. The above verses describe the witnesses clothed in sackcloth, meaning that they will preach of repentance back unto the favor of God (Isaiah 37:1-2; Daniel 9:3-5). These two men who will testify during the end times will be Enoch and Elijah, the two men of God who never knew death but were translated before they had died (Genesis 5:21-24; Malachi

4:5). The book of Revelation states this in Chapter 11 verse 4: "These are the two olive trees and the two candlesticks standing before the God of the Earth". This is a reference to Zechariah Chapter 4. These men will preach the truth unto the nations and will be in direct opposition of the Anti-Christ, who will be in control of the majority of the world at that time. The bible states that after their three and a half year ministry, they will be murdered by Anti-Christ by way of the Beast from the Bottomless Pit in Revelation 11:7. This states: "And when they shall have finished their testimony, the beast that ascendeth out of the bottomless pit shall make war against them, and shall overcome them, and kill them."

The Bible goes on to say in verses 8-10:

And their dead bodies shall lie in the street of the great city, which spiritually is called Sodom and Egypt, where also our Lord was crucified. And they of the people and kindreds and tongues and nations shall see their dead bodies three days and an half, and shall not suffer their dead bodies to be put in graves. And they that dwell upon the earth shall rejoice over them, and make merry, and shall send gifts one to another; because these two prophets tormented them that dwelt on the Earth.

This testifies to the evilness of the unredeemed in the last days, which will rejoice at the death of the men of God. This will teach the truth of the Holy scriptures as happy and sharing of gifts. We can see this happening even today, as good men and women are deemed judgmental heretics when they preach against sin and what the Word of God actually says, which is that repentance is necessary to be washed in the blood of Christ. The scripture goes on to say in Revelation 11 and 12:

And after three days and an half the spirit of life from God entered into them, and they stood upon their feet; and great fear fell upon them which saw them. And they heard a great voice from heaven saying unto them, Come up hither. And they ascended up to heaven in a cloud; and their enemies beheld them.

We know that teaching the Word of God is not always met with praise and thankfulness, but at times with opposition and hardships. As we approach the last days, say faithful to the scriptures and proclaim truly what it says. That even though we may be shunned of this world, God will always raise us up to be glorified through Christ.

The Great White Throne Judgment

And I saw a great white throne, and him that sat on it, from whose face the earth and the heaven fled away; and there was found no place for them. And I saw the dead, small and great, stand before God; and the books were opened: and another book was opened, which is the book of life: and the dead were judged out of those things which were written in the books, according to their works. And the sea gave up the dead which were in it; and death and hell delivered up the dead which were in them: and they were judged every man according to their works. And death and hell were cast into the lake of fire. This is the second death. And whosoever was not found written in the book of life was cast into the lake of fire. – Revelation 20:11-15

The Great White Throne Judgement of God, spoken of here in the book of Revelation 20:11-15, is the final judgment prior to the unsaved being cast into the Lake of Fire. This will take place right after the Millenium Reign of Christ, also known as The Kingdom Age (this being the time in which The Glorified Christ will return and cast the False Prophet and the Anti Christ into the Lake of Fire as read in Revelation 19:20).

And the beast was taken, and with him the false prophet that wrought miracles before him, with which he deceived them that had received the mark of the beast, and them that worshipped his image. These both were cast alive into a lake of fire burning with brimstone.

After this time, Christ will reign for a thousand years over the Earth, but will still have arrogant nonbelievers here present with Him on Earth, denying who

He is. It is at this time that Satan will be released by God to persuade these nonbelievers into throwing in their lot with Him in one last attempt to destroy Christ. But this is really the Lord's way of finally cleansing the world of all who reject Him and His plan for Salvation. Revelation 20: 7-9 reads:

> *And when the thousand years are expired, Satan shall be loosed out of his prison, And shall go out to deceive the nations which are in the four quarters of the earth, Gog, and Magog, to gather them together to battle: the number of whom is as the sand of the sea. And they went up on the breadth of the earth, and compassed the camp of the saints about, and the beloved city: and fire came down from God out of heaven, and devoured them.*

At this time Jesus will totally do away with every unrighteous person and Satan forever in the World, leaving only Christ and the Children of God to reign with Him forever. It is at this time that the final judgment will begin with the Book of Life being opened and everyone living and dead individual who ever lived will be judged. They will receive life with Christ or the judgment of fire by refusing to repent for their sins. I pray that will all stay active in promoting the gospel of Jesus Christ, so that on the day of the Great White Throne Judgment, all our loved one's names are found written in the Book of Life

As in the Days of Noah

But as the days of Noah were, so shall also the coming of the Son of man be. – Matthew 24:37-38

To best understand the end times, one must only look to the true Word of God, the Holy Bible. The Bible is the only true source of God among all the false religions of the world. This bible predicts the total end times, which proves it legitimate as God's Word. The Holy Spirit of God would never leave us blind to upcoming events that predict the return of the Christ in those very troublesome days. Jesus told His followers that the time before His return "will be as in the days of Noah," (Matthew 24:37-38). Those were great days of wickedness upon mankind, where as even mankind's very thoughts were of evil, as stated in Genesis 6:5. The coming of the end times can be seen played out before our very eyes everyday on our national news channels. But Matthew 24:37-38 also alludes to a very dangerous prophecy; that of "The Sons of God", the Watchers.

Genesis 6:4 states the reason for the flood: "There were giants in the Earth in those days; and also after that, when the sons of God came in unto the daughters of men, and they bare children to them, the same became mighty men which were of old, men of renown." These were fallen angels who left their heavenly estate to aid Satan in polluting the human bloodline in an attempt to stop the birth of the messiah Jesus Christ. The Fallen Angels tried to thwart Him by introducing a non-human entity into the gene pool of mankind. Satan meant to stop the plan that God set in motion in Genesis 3:14-15, which reads:

And the LORD God said unto the serpent, Because thou hast done this, thou art cursed above all cattle, and above every beast of the field; upon thy belly shalt thou go, and dust shalt thou eat all the days of thy life: And I will put enmity between thee and the woman, and between thy seed and her seed; it shall bruise thy head, and thou shalt bruise his heel.

Her seed in this verse speaks of Mary bruising the head of Satan by producing the Christ. The Watchers (fallen angels) was a name given by Enoch who was the great grandfather of Noah and son of Jared (Genesis 5:18). This name greatly describes these beings in His extra Biblical text "The Book of Enoch." The early church excluded this book from the Bible because they believed it to be heresy that man and angels could conceive offspring, even though the bible clearly states otherwise in Genesis 6:4. In the last days these fallen angels (Watchers) will return to continue their plan of corruption and to aid the Anti-Christ in His plan of obtaining a one world religion. This will help Him receive worship which will cause a great falling away from the Christian faith, as stated in 2 Thessalonians 2:3. The books of Job 1:6; 2:1 and Jude 6:7 support Enoch's claims of just what these beings did. Their return is imminent, as recorded in Revelation 11:8 and Revelation 17:8, in which he is referred to as "beast."

I believe what people are seeing and experiencing today as "aliens" or UFOs are actually these fallen angels or Nephilim, whom abductees claim to undergo similar experiments by these so-called "aliens". This is much as the Watchers did in a time past and after, seeing as how the bible states they were present after the flood in Genesis 6:4. The unfolding of these events should not concern any Christian believer because Jesus said these things will come to pass before His return. Keep your faith on Christ and Christ only in spite of the circumstances around you. We are more than conquers through Him. Christ will see us through every ungodly event just as He did for Noah.

Apollyon the Fallen Angel of the Bottomless Pit

And they had a king over them, which is the angel of the bottomless pit, whose name in the Hebrew tongue is Abaddon, but in the Greek tongue hath his name Apollyon. – Revelation 9:11, "

The ninth chapter of the book of Revelations gives us a revealing look into the Spirit realm, which will greatly affect the natural world as we know it. Here Saint John is given a glimpse of the release of the "Destroyer". Abaddon, or Apollyon in Greek, is the very powerful fallen angel who will greatly assist the Anti-Christ in the coming end times. There are only four angels mentioned by name in the Holy Bible, with each being very significant. Apollyon is the conquering fallen angel who will establish the New World Order or One World Government, in which the false Christ will reign over to persecute Israel. This New World Government will be a re-birth of the Greek Empire; the same one that Alexander the Great ruled over with the help of this same fallen angel, as read in Revelation 13:2-3:

> *And the beast which I saw was like unto a leopard, and his feet were as the feet of a bear, and his mouth as the mouth of a lion: and the dragon gave him his power, and his*

seat, and great authority. And I saw one of his heads as it were wounded to death; and his deadly wound was healed: and all the world wondered after the beast.

The "beast" spoken of here is Apollyon. "One of his heads" wounded doesn't relate to the Antichrist, but to one of the Empires from the past, namely the Roman Empire. That "deadly wound" being "healed" means the reestablishment of the empire. This government is mentioned in Revelation 13:7: "And it was given unto him to make war with the saints, and to overcome them: and power was given him over all kindreds, and tongues, and nations."

Apollyon will be a great deceiver to the world, giving false doctrine and hope to all mankind who worship the Antichrist. Apollyon will gain access to the world's media to demonically influence every nonbeliever. He will also have strength and force to dominate and destroy, as read by His murder of the two witnesses in Revelation 11:7: "And when they shall have finished their testimony, the beast that ascendeth out of the bottomless pit shall make war against them, and shall overcome them, and kill them." It is important throughout Apollyon's release that we as believers stay prayerful and not fall away from the faith of our Lord Jesus Christ. We need to stay in His word the Holy Bible so that we can recognize these events and relay the truth unto the rest of the world. As Christians, we will be the only ones who will not believe the lie of Satan, as stated in Revelation 13:8-9: " And all that dwell upon the Earth shall worship him, whose names are NOT written in the book of life of the Lamb slain from the foundation of the world. If any man have an ear, let him hear."

The Word of God says that all will worship Him except for Christians since our names are written in the Book of Life. This only happens if we stand with Christ in these times; recognize, hear and speak the truth to others. The bible says, "Let any man have an ear, let him hear."

The Unforgiveable Sin

"Wherefore I say unto you, All manner of sin and blasphemy shall be forgiven unto men: but the blasphemy against the Holy Ghost shall not be forgiven unto men. And whosoever speaketh a word against the Son of man, it shall be forgiven him: but whosoever speaketh against the Holy Ghost, it shall not be forgiven him, neither in this world, neither in the world to come. – Matthew 12:31-32

The Holy Bible speaks of a time when many believers will be delivered up to the Anti-Christ to give a testimony on the behalf of the Lord Jesus Christ, proclaiming that He is the one true Son of God. Jesus made reference to this event three times, in scripture Matthew 12:31-32, Mark 3:29, and Luke 12:10. At this time in front of a world audience, the Holy Spirit will overcome the Christian believer and speak the true Word of God for all who have ears to hear. Hopefully, all will repent before the second coming of our Lord. This overcoming of the Holy Spirit will not be forced, but will come to Christian only if they allow it. Those who allow the Spirit of God to speak through them will reach many with the Gospel of Jesus Christ and allow the lost to overcome the coming tribulations. Those who do not are denying God the opportunity to bring many back unto Him by way of hearing the testimony of Jesus Christ. Jesus described this sin as unforgivable to those true believers who say they follow Christ. In doing so they deny His Holy Spirit to speak through them in the presence of the Beast. Please know that this sin can *only* be committed by those who profess Jesus Christ as the true Savior. It does not apply to those who have no reference of Jesus Christ as God.

So who will deny God the opportunity to witness to millions in front of the Devil incarnate? I believe many weak Christians will, as we can attest from popular pastors who deny Christ as the only way when being interviewed on major news stations. This is not to mention many churchgoers who refuse to share Christ with co-workers and friends on the belief that they may be rejected or ridiculed. I ask that every Christian share the gospel regardless of the circumstances in front of all. All Christians should allow the Holy Spirit to move through them to convert others! It will build our faith in the Lord and prepare those who are chosen to speak. It will give all the strength and courage to testify and convert many.

The 7 Seals of Revelations

And I saw when the Lamb opened one of the seals, and I heard, as it were the noise of thunder, one of the four beasts saying, Come and see. – Revelation 6:1

The discerning of the times we live in is very important to every believer in the Christian faith to understand. This is for us to be able to see and warn people while preparing ourselves for the coming tribulations. This will aid our eventual rapture of the Church of Christ. The book of Revelation is very clear on the events that will lead into the Kingdom Age of Christ. The first is the revealing of the seven Seals. The beginning of the end (the tribulation period) begins with the revealing of the great mystery of God. Only the Lamb of God (Jesus) is the one justified and uncorrupted to open the seven Seals to end this Earth Age. The 1st Seal opened in Revelation 6:1-2, states:

And I saw when the Lamb opened one of the seals, and I heard, as it were the noise of thunder, one of the four beasts saying, Come and see. And I saw, and behold a white horse: and he that sat on him had a bow; and a crown was given unto him: and he went forth conquering, and to conquer.

This "white horse" is symbolic of the Anti-Christ, who while enter the world stage and present Himself as a peacekeeper. But He will reveal Himself to be something much worse. The "bow" indicates that he will speak peace but plot war with the "crown", which represents His many conquered nations. The 2nd Seal opened in Revelation 6:3-4 reads:

And when he had opened the second seal, I heard the second beast say, Come and see. And there went out another horse that was red: and power was given to him that sat thereon to take peace from the earth, and that they should kill one another: and there was given unto him a great sword.

The "red horse" represents war and "power given unto Him" means the Anti-Christ will be given authority to destroy many at this time. The 3rd Seal opened in verse 6:5-6 reveals:

And when he had opened the third seal, I heard the third beast say, Come and see. And I beheld, and lo a black horse; and he that sat on him had a pair of balances in his hand. And I heard a voice in the midst of the four beasts say, A measure of wheat for a penny, and three measures of barley for a penny; and see thou hurt not the oil and the wine.

The "black horse" here is famine and the balances are symbolic of little or no food being available to those in this part of the world, and the grave cost of each. The 4th Seal in Revelations 6:7-8 states:

> *And when he had opened the fourth seal, I heard the voice of the fourth beast say, Come and see. And I looked, and behold a pale horse: and his name that sat on him was Death, and Hell followed with him. And power was given unto them over the fourth part of the earth, to kill with sword, and with hunger, and with death, and with the beasts of the earth.*

The "pale horse" is revealed to be death, meaning all those who had been slain at this time are destined for Hell. The 5th Seal in Revelation 6:9-11 states:

And when he had opened the fifth seal, I saw under the altar the souls of them that were slain for the word of God, and for the testimony which they held: And they cried with a loud voice, saying, How long, O Lord, holy and true, dost thou not judge and avenge our blood on them that dwell on the Earth? And white robes were given unto every one of them; and it was said unto them, that they should rest yet for a little season, until their fellow servants also and their brethren, that should be killed as they were, should be fulfilled.

The 5th Seal speaks of the Christians martyred for their faith at this time. They will pray for judgment on the Lawless one (Anti-Christ) for His actions at this time, which will soon be carried out by God. The 6th Seal in Revelation 6: 12-17 states:

And I beheld when he had opened the sixth seal, and, lo, there was a great earthquake; and the sun became black as sackcloth of hair, and the moon became as blood; And the stars of heaven fell unto the earth, even as a fig tree casteth her untimely figs, when she is shaken of a mighty wind. And the heaven departed as a scroll when it is rolled together; and every mountain and island were moved out of their places. And the kings of the Earth, and the great men, and the rich men, and the chief captains, and the mighty men, and every bondman, and every free man, hid themselves in the dens and in the rocks of the mountains; And said to the mountains and rocks, Fall on us, and hide us from the face of him that sitteth on the throne, and from the wrath of the

Lamb: For the great day of his wrath is come; and who shall be able to stand?

This represents the first of many earthquakes upon the Earth, which will result in the sun being blotted out from the dust of the land. This will be followed by meteorite showers falling upon the Earth, causing severe damage similar to that of Sodom and Gomorrah. After this time, the restoration of Israel will begin along with the tribulation Saints, who gave their lives during this time. They will cry and thank Jesus for their salvation.

The 7th Seal in Revelation 8:1-6 reads:

And when he had opened the seventh seal, there was silence in heaven about the space of half an hour. And I saw the seven angels which stood before God; and to them were given seven trumpets. And another angel came and stood at the altar, having a golden censer;

and there was given unto him much incense, that he should offer it with the prayers of all saints upon the golden altar which was before the throne. And the smoke of the incense, which came with the prayers of the saints, ascended up before God out of the angel's hand. And the angel took the censer, and filled it with fire of the altar, and cast it into the earth: and there were voices, and thunderings, and lightnings, and an earthquake. And the seven angels which had the seven trumpets prepared themselves to sound.

The 7th Seal represents the judgment of God, with the seven angels representing the presence of God, which will begin the seven trumpet judgments. The angels fill the Golden Censer (vessels made for burning incense) with the incense of the perfect virtue of Jesus Christ and His once and perfect sacrifice at the Cross. This will be offered up with the prayers of all who believe and pray to God, who hears all and will ascend up before Jehovah. He will then cast to the Earth, which will signify the judgment of God, within three years of the great tribulation.

The 7 Trumpets of Revelations

So the seven angels who had the seven trumpets prepared themselves to sound. – Revelations 8:6 (NKJV)

Soon after the opening of the 7 Seals of Revelations, the seven trumpets of judgment will sound upon the Earth. The 1st trumpet (Revelation 8:7) will bring about great destruction upon the land. This is very similar to the seventh plague upon Egypt in Exodus 9:22, which mainly affects the Middle East and a great part of the rest of the world. This destruction upon the vegetation of the Earth will be a fulfillment of a prophecy found in Joel 2:30-32. The 2nd trumpet will cause a "great burning mountain" to be cast into the sea (Revelation 8:8-9). This "great mountain" will be a meteorite, which will fall from space to contaminate the Earth's body of waters, causing a discoloration of the sea and causing death of much of the sea life in the world. The 3rd trumpet (Revelation 8:10) sounded by the Angels of God will cause another meteorite to fall to the Earth by the name wormwood. Wormwood was a toxic plant from the Old Testament found in Jeremiah 9:15 (NKJV), which reads: "therefore thus says the LORD of hosts, the God of Israel: 'Behold, I will feed them, this people, with wormwood, and give them water of gall to drink.'"

This contamination of the Earth's water will cause mass death in the surrounding area. The 4th trumpet is described in Revelation 8:12-13 (NKJV), which reads;

Then the fourth angel sounded: And a third of the sun was struck, a third of the moon, and a third of the stars, so that a third of them were darkened. A third of the day did not shine, and likewise the night. And I looked, and I heard an angel flying through the midst of heaven, saying with a loud voice, "Woe, woe, woe to the inhabitants of the earth, because of the remaining blasts of the trumpet of the three angels who are about to sound!"

The blocking out of the sun always represents a strong judgment handed out by God, as foretold by Jesus in Luke 21:25-26. The three "woes" represent the last three trumpets to sound upon the Earth. The 5th trumpet in Revelations 9:1-4 (NKJV) reads:

Then the fifth angel sounded: And I saw a star fallen from heaven to the Earth. To him was given the key to the bottomless pit. And he opened the bottomless pit, and smoke arose out of the pit like the smoke of a great furnace. So the sun and the air were darkened because of the smoke of the pit. Then out of the smoke locusts came upon the earth. And to them was given power, as the scorpions of the earth have power. They were commanded not to harm the grass of the earth, or any green thing, or any tree, but only those men who do not have the seal of God on their foreheads.

The falling star here is Satan, who is cast out of Heaven in order to open the bottomless pit. Satan will release demonic spirit in the form of locusts and scorpions upon those who chose the Anti-Christ instead of Christ in the end times. God gives orders to not destroy the land but those who have the seal of the Beast on their foreheads. This will be a great time of torment upon the unsaved, who believed a lie instead of the truth of Jesus Christ. Revelations 9:6 says many will seek death but will not find it at this time. This shows the end result of disobedience toward God. The 6th trumpet (Revelation 9:13-21) represents the second woe of the angel of God. At this time, four powerful evil fallen angels will be released from the Euphrates river to execute God's wrath. These evil angels command an army of some 200 thousand thousand (or 200 million), who will be responsible for the deaths of a third of mankind.

The 7th trumpet (Revelation 1:15-19) is the final "woe" signaled by the angel of God. This will come at last three and a half years into the tribulation in which the twenty elders on the throne proclaim Jesus Christ as Lord. His judgment has come to those who chose the side of the Anti-Christ during the great tribulation and the Will of the Father has been done. This will deliver those who denied Christ to their final fate of separation from God into Hell.

The 7 Bowls of Revelations

"Then I heard a loud voice from the temple saying to the seven angels, "Go and pour out the bowls (Vials) of the wrath of God on the Earth. – Revelation 16:1 (NKJV)

Once the 7 Seals and 7 Trumpets of God have sounded, the 7 bowl judgments will begin. This judgment will be on the population of the world, who has rejected the Gospel of Jesus Christ and received the mark of the Beast (see blogs under End Times Prophecy for explanation of both). The 1st judgment of the ungodly will be a similar affliction given to the Egyptians in Exodus 9:9-11. It will be in the form of painful sores according to Revelation 16:2. The 2nd Bowl, which is found Revelation 16:3 (NKJV), states: "Then the second angel poured out his bowl on the sea, and it became blood as of a dead man; and every living creature in the sea died." This will affect a third of the Earth seas, killing much of the sea life therein. The 3rd bowl will be of the entire water source on Earth, as found in Revelation 16:4-7(NKJV), which states:

> *Then the third angel poured out his bowl on the rivers and springs of water, and they became blood. And I heard the angel of the waters saying: "You are righteous, O Lord, The One who is and who was and who is to be, Because You have judged these things For they have shed the blood of saints and prophets, And You have given them blood to drink. For it is their just due." And I heard another from the altar saying, "Even so, Lord God Almighty, true and righteous are Your judgments."*

The 4th bowl will scorch men and women who have blasphemed God. This judgment is particularly brutal given the fact that God has given the world thousands of years to except His plan for salvation. However, they have refused and curse Him for it. The 5th Bowl will be against the Satan's Kingdom of the New World Order. The powers of darkness, who have ruled the Earth throughout time such, will suffer this plague. The 6th Bowl will dry up the Euphrates River and present a straightaway for the Kings of the East to be gathered by way of the Unholy Trinity of Satan, the false Prophet, and the Beast. Revelation 16: 12-16 (NKJV) states:

> *Then the sixth angel poured out his bowl on the great river Euphrates, and its water was dried up, so that the way of the kings from the east might be prepared. And I saw three unclean spirits like frogs coming out of the mouth of the dragon, out of the mouth of the beast, and out of the mouth of the false prophet. For they are spirits of demons,*

performing signs, which go out to the kings of the earth and[a] of the whole world, to gather them to the battle of that great day of God Almighty. "Behold, I am coming as a thief. Blessed is he who watches, and keeps his garments, lest he walk naked and they see his shame. "And they gathered them together to the place called in Hebrew, Armageddon.

The final 7th judgment will be the last before the return of Christ. This bowl consists of great earthquakes and hail from heaven, which shake the foundation of the world. Revelation 16:17-21 states:

Then the seventh angel poured out his bowl into the air, and a loud voice came out of the temple of heaven, from the throne, saying, "It is done!" And there were noises and thunderings and lightnings; and there was a great earthquake, such a mighty and great earthquake as had not occurred since men were on the earth. Now the great city was divided into three parts, and the cities of the nations fell. And great Babylon was remembered before God, to give her the cup of the wine of the fierceness of His wrath. Then every island fled away, and the mountains were not found. And great hail from heaven fell upon men, each hailstone about the weight of a talent. Men blasphemed God because of the plague of the hail, since that plague was exceedingly great.

The Satanic Empires of these times will be reduced to rubble and bring about an end to the New World Order of the end time. These judgments on the behalf of God are righteous in their use. Regardless of how one reads and interprets the actions of the Most High, God is still a God of love. These judgments are for the unsaved and satanic children of this world, who have rejected love and grace for the pleasures of this world. I pray that we all are productive ministers of the cross of Christ, and hopefully save many from this fate by accepting the Lord Jesus Christ. Soon after the 7 Bowls of Revelations, the return of Christ will mark the defeat of Satan and the beginning of the new Earth age. The book of Revelation Chapter 21:1-8(NKJV) reads:

Now I saw a new heaven and a new Earth, for the first heaven and the first earth had passed away. Also there was no more sea. Then I, John, saw the holy city, New Jerusalem, coming down out of heaven from God, prepared as a bride adorned for her husband. And I heard a loud voice from heaven saying, "Behold, the tabernacle of God is with men, and He will dwell with them, and they shall be His people. God Himself will be with them and be their God. And God will wipe away every tear from their eyes; there shall be no more death, nor sorrow, nor crying. There shall be no more pain, for the former things have passed away." Then He who sat on the throne said, "Behold, I make all things new." And He said to me, "Write, for these words are true and faithful." And He said to me, "It is done! I am the Alpha and the Omega, the Beginning and the End. I will give of the fountain of the water of life freely to him who thirsts. He who overcomes shall inherit all things, and I will be his God and he shall be My son. But the cowardly, unbelieving, abominable, murderers, sexually immoral, sorcerers, idolaters, and all liars shall have their part in the lake which burns with fire and brimstone, which is the second death.

There is one way – and only ONE way – to overcome the end tribulation and the adversary. That is by accepting Jesus Christ as Lord and Savior. In receiving the begotten son of God perfect sacrifice, we receive the remission of the sinful nature in us and the grace of God.

Chapter 5

The Redemption of Man

In a moment, in the twinkling of an eye, at the last trumpet. For the trumpet will sound, and the dead will be raised incorruptible, and we shall be changed. For this corruptible must put on incorruption, and this mortal must put on immortality. So when this corruptible has put on incorruption, and this mortal has put on immortality, then shall be brought to pass the saying that is written: "Death is swallowed up in victory." – 1 Corinthians 15:52-54 (NKJV)

The Holy Bible and all of its scripture testify to the coming redemption of man and the Kingdom age of Christ. In the beginning, man was created perfect and in the image of God. He was given dominion over all the Earth. Once Adam and Eve allowed themselves to be given over to sin, all of mankind's domain was handed over to Satan. Mankind received a fallen state and lost the glory of God in his flesh. In this fallen state, man began to age and die. He lost Godful consciousness and gained self-consciousness, which would lead to death. Sin has affected the whole social order of the Earthly world, which was originally created to have a Heavenly ruled government. This is now is ruled by satanic forces and sinful men. The penance for sin has been extremely great for all human beings. Murders, rapes, slavery and holocaust have ravaged the once great land God had given unto man.

Even so, the love God has for us is too great for him to leave or forsake us. Once Adam and Eve inherited the sinful nature from the tree of Good and Evil, (symbolic of Satan and his kingdom), God began his plan for redemption. First, the curse of sin was revealed. Genesis 3:14-24 (NKJV) states:

> *So the Lord God said to the serpent: "Because you have done this, You are cursed more than all cattle, And more than every beast of the field; On your belly you shall go, And you shall eat dust All the days of your life. And I will put enmity Between you and the woman, And between your seed and her Seed; He shall bruise your head, And you shall bruise His heel." To the woman He said: "I will greatly multiply your sorrow and your conception; In pain you shall bring forth children; Your desire shall be for your husband, And he shall rule over you." Then to Adam He said, "Because you have heeded the voice of your wife, and have eaten from the tree of which I commanded you, saying, 'You*

shall not eat of it': "Cursed is the ground for your sake; In toil you shall eat of it All the days of your life. Both thorns and thistles it shall bring forth for you, And you shall eat the herb of the field. In the sweat of your face you shall eat bread till you return to the ground, for out of it you were taken; for dust you are, and to dust you shall return." And Adam called his wife's name Eve, because she was the mother of all living. Also for Adam and his wife the Lord God made tunics of skin, and clothed them. Then the Lord God said, "Behold, the man has become like one of Us, to know good and evil. And now, lest he put out his hand and take also of the tree of life, and eat, and live forever"— therefore the Lord God sent him out of the garden of Eden to till the ground from which he was taken. So

He drove out the man; and He placed cherubim at the east of the garden of Eden, and a flaming sword which turned every way, to guard the way to the tree of life. In the mercy of God in the same breath He revealed a seed that would bruise the head of the Serpent, which is metaphor of Christ and his finished work at the Cross.

The holy scriptures then follow Moses, Abraham, King David and others who headed the word of God and awaited the promised Messiah to redeem mankind. The finished work of the cross, gave man the power to overcome until Jesus Christ return and resist the Devil. The end of this Earth Age culminates at the end of the 7th Bowl of Judgment. The long promised return of the Messiah will come as revealed in Revelations 19:11-16 (NKJV) states:

Now I saw heaven opened, and behold, a white horse. And He who sat on him was called Faithful and True, and in righteousness He judges and makes war. His eyes were like a flame of fire, and on His head were many crowns. He had a name written that no one knew except Himself. He was clothed with a robe dipped in blood, and His name is called The Word of God. And the armies in heaven, clothed in fine linen, white and clean, followed Him on white horses. Now out of His mouth goes a sharp sword, that with it He should strike the nations. And He Himself will rule them with a rod of iron. He Himself treads the winepress of the fierceness and wrath of Almighty God. And He has on His robe and on His thigh a name written: KING OF KINGS AND LORD OF LORDS.

Jesus will overthrow the Anti-Christ and False Prophet and bind Satan for 1,000 years. During this time of

Satan's imprisonment, there will be a great revival of the Church and time of repentance for those still unsaved. God is long suffering for all to come into repentance. He will give those who have not heard the fospel the chance for redemption, as stated in 2 Peter 3:9 (NKJV), which reads: "The Lord is not slack concerning His promise, as some count slackness, but is longsuffering toward us, not willing that any should perish but that all should come to repentance."

After this period, Satan will be released for one last seduction of man, resulting in His fate being sealed and swallowed up by the Lake of Fire. Once the Devil and unredeemed have been done away with, God will reboot the entire Earth purging it by fire and making it anew. 2 Peter 3:7 (NKJV) states: "But the heavens and the Earth which are now preserved by the same word, are reserved for fire until the Day of Judgment and perdition of ungodly men." Jesus Christ will the dwell with us as our King and usher in a new kingdom age of eternal peace, and returning all back into the Garden of Eden on Earth. Shalom…

Chapter 6

Accepting Jesus Christ

As we have read, the Holy Bible reveals that we as men and women have fallen from the perfect image of God in which we were created. The fruit of the Tree of Good and Evil altered the genetic makeup of man, putting us in direct opposition of our creator. The scriptures state that there is only ONE way to be made right, and that is by putting on the perfect nature of the Son of God, Jesus Christ. The power of Christ gives all the ability to endure until the end. He gives us the power to resist Satan, fallen angels, demonic spirits, and evil men. At this time, I would like to offer those who have not received the salvation that is in Jesus Christ the opportunity to do so. Christianity is not a religion of works and ignorant beliefs. It is solely based on building a personal relationship with Jesus, so that when God looks at us, He sees the covering that we wear, which is Christ. John 3:16 reads: "For God loved the world so much that he gave his one and only Son, so that everyone who believes in him will not perish but have eternal life." If you truly put forth all your faith in the Lord Jesus and in the cross of Christ, God will grant you salvation and redeem your soul. Confess this with Me:

Lord Jesus, I need you. Thank You for dying on the cross for my sins. I open the door of my life and receive you as my Savior and Lord. Thank You for forgiving my sins and giving me eternal life. Take control of the throne of my life. Make me the kind of person you want me to be. Amen...

Once you have confessed this with your heart, eternal salvation is now yours. Find a good bible-based church and confess your faith to others that Jesus Christ is Lord and is the only way…

About the Author

Rosey V Summerville was born in the small city of Fairbanks, Alaska. He is currently serving in the United States Air Force and has been receiving biblical training since his young childhood. In 2006, Rosey received the calling to Minister the Gospel of Jesus Christ and began studying and researching specific topics of the Holy Bible. On February 2, 2009, he was ordained a Minister into Christian clergy, with this book being the second of his ministry. I hope all are blessed by each and every chapter in *The Gospel: The Teachings, Teachings and Prophecy of the Messiah.*

Visit www.divinegospelministry.net for weekly postings on the Gospel of Jesus Christ.

www.ingramcontent.com/pod-product-compliance
Lightning Source LLC
LaVergne TN
LVHW020926090426
835512LV00020B/3215